Psychological Biblical Criticism

Psychological Biblical Criticism

by D. Andrew Kille

Minneapolis

PSYCHOLOGICAL BIBLICAL CRITICISM

Library of Congress Cataloging-in-Publication Data

Kille, D. Andrew.
Psychological biblical criticism / D. Andrew Kille.
p. cm. — (Guides to biblical scholarship. Old Testament series)
Includes bibliographical references.
ISBN 0-8006-3246-X (alk paper)
1. Bible. O.T.—Psychology. 2. Bible. O.T.—Criticism, interpretation, etc. I. Title. II. Series.

BS1199.P9 K55 2000
221.6'01'9—dc21 00-048401

The paper used in this publication meets the minimum requirements of American National Standard for Information Sciences—Permanence of Paper for Printed Library Materials, ANSI Z329.48-1984.

Manufactured in the U.S.A. AF 1-3246
05 04 03 02 01 1 2 3 4 5 6 7 8 9 10

To Pam

"Therefore a man leaves his father and mother and clings to his wife, and they become one flesh."

—Genesis 2:24

Contents

Foreword

Psychological language and presuppositions are deeply embedded in contemporary culture. Since the time of Freud in particular, we have been increasingly concerned with the internal life of individuals, with emotions, feelings, motivations, their causes and their effects. Indeed, one could argue that a leading theme if not the defining concern of modern western culture is the human psyche. The modern novel, in virtually all its forms, is just one example of literature that focuses upon psychological forces that are seen to shape individuals and plots.

Psychological interests abound in scholarly circles as well and certainly are not limited to the disciplines of psychology and psychiatry. The historian wants to know not only the sequence of events but what was going on in the minds and hearts of the leading characters. It should not be surprising, therefore, that biblical scholarship should turn to psychological interpretation.

In the volume before us, Andrew Kille traces the history of psychological approaches to the Bible beginning with Freud and his contemporaries, but recognizing that concern with psychological factors was even present in antiquity. As he points out, the history of modern work in this arena has been mixed, ranging from Freud's reductionism to efforts to psychoanalyze ancient characters to significant and substantial contributions to the understanding of biblical texts.

Kille sets out a definition not of a psychological method as such but of an approach to biblical interpretation, including criteria for evaluating the application of such approaches. Using Genesis 3 as a point of departure and a test case, he shows how a variety of works have or have not produced valuable and distinctive interpretations. So in addition to showing how psychological approaches function, this volume includes important contributions to the interpretation of a biblical text that is a key to understanding how the Bible has shaped human self-understanding.

In this book Kille shows that psychological interpretation is not limited to scholars who would identify themselves by such a label, but that it is visible in the work of a wide range of biblical interpreters. These include feminist readings and some forms of literary analysis. Consequently, the understanding of psychological approaches and their contributions is important in itself, but also for comprehending other developments in biblical interpretation as well.

—Gene M. Tucker

Preface

When I first began my studies in psychological biblical criticism in the late 1980's I was often asked "You are getting a degree in *what*?" There was no established field at that time, and when I would explain my studies I would receive contrasting responses. Folks outside the discipline of biblical studies would find it fascinating and exciting. Comments from those within the academy ranged from "Sounds interesting. Is there really any literature on that?" to "I've never been much interested in that stuff. I don't find it very helpful," to some variation on the comment made by Robin Scroggs's erstwhile professor: "Bultmann taught us years ago to be suspicious of psychology" (1982).

My journey into the intersections of psychology and biblical studies began accidentally. A book club mistakenly sent me Morton Kelsey's *The Other Side of Silence* (Paulist, 1976). Kelsey's book intrigued me and led me to John Sanford's work, and then to workshops with Walter Wink and Kelsey. As I have moved deeper into psychological biblical criticism, the path has been marked by many such "accidents" (Jung would call them synchronistic). Many times I have met just the right person at the right time, and I am grateful not only to those people, but to the circumstances that made it possible for me to know and work with them.

I began my work knowing little of what I faced. My interest in psychological criticism had developed over several years as a pastor working closely with mental health practitioners, most notably my wife, who is a clinical psychologist. I found Jungian psychology compelling, particularly as brought to bear on the biblical text by John Sanford, Wayne Rollins, Walter Wink, and Elizabeth Howes. I participated in seminars led by Howes's group in San Francisco, the Guild for Psychological Studies, which for years has held seminars combining critical study of the synoptic Gospels with Jungian psychology.

For all that I appreciated the psychological insights of various writers, I was deeply concerned about their frequent lack of awareness of basic issues in biblical studies. I felt a need to discover a more adequate and comprehensive approach, and so it was with no little naïveté that I began to look for a school at which I could study psychological criticism. No such program existed; fortunately, the Graduate Theological Union in Berkeley proved flexible enough to enable me to create one.

My initial proposal to study psychological hermeneutics included questions that remain relevant: What insight does a theory of personality bring to biblical texts? What are the limits of a psychological approach? How can one hold the particularity and universality of a text in their proper tension?

Few of the biblical studies faculty at that time were interested in working specifically with psychological approaches. One notable exception was Wilhelm Wuellner of the Pacific School of Religion. Wuellner described the hostility he had encountered from his colleagues when he and Robert Leslie published *The Surprising Gospel* in 1984. He and Valerie DeMarinis, who was teaching Pastoral Care at PSR, had attempted once or twice to bring together students in biblical studies and pastoral counseling, but had been unable to develop any momentum for ongoing conversation. One invaluable resource that Wuellner shared with me was an extensive bibliography on psychological biblical criticism, which gave me a starting point for my own investigations.

Lewis Rambo of the San Francisco Theological Seminary became a second guiding light, guiding my reading in the psychology of religion. By another happy coincidence, I met Wayne Rollins in a class on Depth Psychology while he was on sabbatical in residence at the GTU. I am grateful to Prof. Rollins for the stimulating and encouraging conversations we have had over the years, and his presence on my comprehensive and dissertation committees. His thoughtful critiques and vision of the potential contributions of psychological criticism have had crucial impact on my evolving work. In addition, Rollins's efforts on behalf of a newly-emerging field of psychological criticism have provided a home for me and others in the wider discipline. His contributions have included organizing and developing the Psychology and Biblical Studies

Program Unit of the Society of Biblical Literature from Consultation to Group to Section in just a few years.

Equipped with bibliographies from Wuellner, Rollins, and Rambo, I delved deeply into psychological biblical criticism. Two facts struck me: far more literature existed than anyone had suspected, and it was chaotic. Neither biblical scholars nor psychologists of religion are familiar with much of the literature.

In looking to the future of psychological criticism, I believe the greatest need at present is to bring greater visibility and coherence to the field, enabling cumulative advancement as new scholars build on previous work. The hit-and-run quality of psychological criticism can only be corrected by cumulative efforts, grounded in theoretical reflection and familiar with a broad span of research.

First, we must make the already considerable body of literature more accessible. The bibliographies compiled by Wuellner and Rollins proved invaluable to me in opening an avenue of approach. Rollins's bibliography is now available as part of his book *Soul and Psyche: The Bible in Psychological Perspective* (Fortress Press, 1999). Beyond simple bibliographic lists, collections of representative work are needed. Such collections might gather examples of interpretation from within a single theoretical orientation, as in *Jung and the Interpretation of the Bible* (David L. Miller, editor; Yale Univ. Press, 1995), or use different theories on a single text, as in the present volume.

Critical and methodological reflection on and analysis of psychological criticism must take place alongside anthologies. Methodological works like *The Postmodern Bible* (The Bible and Culture Collective, 1995) have included psychological criticism in their surveys of critical methods. Rollins's *Soul and Psyche* offers both historical and thematic surveys to bring coherence to the field.

Much of the literature to date has appeared in psychological journals or journals devoted to pastoral psychology. There is a need for journals in biblical studies to be open to publishing new work in the field and allow for discussion and development of ongoing work. The journal *Biblical Interpretation* (Brill), edited by professors at Sheffield University, has already proved its willingness to do just that.

Meanwhile, there is a need for practitioners of psychological biblical criticism to stay in conversation with each other. The Psychology and Biblical

Studies Section of the Society of Biblical Literature and the Person, Culture and Religion Group of the American Academy of Religion serve to keep the work of psychological criticism visible and provide opportunities for mutual support and conversation. In these days of the World Wide Web there is remarkable new potential for continuing the conversation, and for making on-going work accessible to a wider audience via electronic linkages. See my own Web site with resources for psychological criticism at: http://home.att.net/~revdak.

I know that I could not possibly thank all those that I consciously know have helped me along this journey, and am aware that so many others have unconsciously been a part of this effort. I am grateful to Elizabeth Boyden Howes and the Guild for Psychological Studies, who have for many years worked with bringing Jungian psychology to bear on reading the synoptic Gospels, and especially to Guild leaders Manuel Costa and Jerry Drino for numerous seminars, reflections and conversations along the way.

Walter Wink has been not only an inspiring model, but personally supportive and encouraging. Several faculty members at the Graduate Theological Union have made significant contributions to my work. I am grateful to Wilhelm Wuellner for several encouraging conversations early in my program, and especially for his gracious sharing of the bibliography of psychology and biblical studies that he had compiled. Robert B. Coote held me to my commitment to be a credible biblical scholar. Herman Waetjen first introduced me to hermeneutics and literary theory, and especially the work of Paul Ricoeur, and Joel Green challenged me to ground myself solidly in hermeneutic theory.

Lewis Rambo provided invaluable direction for an independent study of the psychology of religion that led to my initial efforts to identify and understand psychological biblical criticism, and we have continued the conversation along the way. Diane Jonte-Pace of Santa Clara University who also came to this project by "accident" proved to be unfailingly gracious and sympathetic; she found time even in the most hectic situations to inquire about my progress and offer her critique and encouragement.

Most of all, I am indebted to Gina Hens-Piazza who guided the writing of the dissertation which provides the core of the present work. It was yet another grace-filled "accident" that led to discovering that she was not only a most capable biblical scholar, but had a background in psychology and an appreciation for the potential contributions of psychological criticism. It was a pleasure to work with Dr. Hens-Piazza as she proved both most gracious and consistently rigorous in challenging me to think clearly through this project. She was unfailingly supportive, readily sharing her time and professional expertise.

Thanks to Fortress Press for the contributions they have already made to psychological biblical criticism with the publication of Rollins's book, and to my editor at Fortress Press, K. C. Hanson, for his suggestions and assistance. Thanks also to Gene M. Tucker, series editor, for accepting this volume in the Guides to Biblical Scholarship series.

Finally, I want to thank my family. My grandmother, Margaret Russell Kille, and my parents, David and Ruth Kille, taught me to love the Bible and to use my head. My sons Jabin and Russell grew up with this project. Russell began kindergarten the same day I began my formal studies and is now one of my proofreaders.

Above all, I want to thank my wife, Dr. Pamela A. Bjorklund. Not only has she supported me materially and emotionally through the process, her professional expertise as a clinical psychologist has provided an important practical context for my theoretical intuitions. Truly, I could not have done it without her.

The past several years have been challenging, maddening and exciting. Many questions remain unanswered; many have yet to be asked. Yet I count it a great honor to find myself among those who are drawn to this newly emergent field.

1 What Is Psychological Biblical Criticism?

The seeming simplicity of the phrase "psychology and the Bible" masks a dizzying complexity. No sooner do we utter the words than we must ask *which* psychology? *What* dimension(s) of the Bible? and *How* do they relate to each other? Although there have been a multitude of efforts to use psychology as a tool to interpret the Bible, it is only recently that a field of psychological biblical criticism has begun to re-emerge.

Psychological approaches to the Bible are not new. The roots of "biblical psychology" extend as far back into church history as the writings of Tertullian and Augustine. Psychology itself began as a subdiscipline of theology; the term *psychology* was coined in the sixteenth century to describe, along with natural theology, angelography, and demonology, the three branches of pneumatology, or the doctrine of spirits. Shortly after, the term *anthropology* was created to refer to the science of persons, having the subdivisions of psychology (science of mind) and somatology (the science of the body) (Vande Kemp 1986:98).

One representative textbook on contemporary psychology defines the field in this way: "*Psychology* is the science that studies behavior—the actions, mental processes, and experiences of humans and other organisms. Any personal activity, whether shown outwardly or experienced inwardly, qualifies as a *behavior*" (Saccuzzo 1987:4). While many often understand psychology to be study of the mind or mental processes, one can study those processes only in reference to observable behavior.

The study of the Bible brings one into contact with human behavior in many ways. Writing, editing, transmission, and interpretation of biblical texts all warrant examination. In its pages, the Bible offers still more material—

descriptions of actions, conversations, and experiences, personalities, and relationships. It is no wonder that a persistent but elusive strand of biblical interpretation has sought to bring the insights of psychological theory to bear on the text. This strand, however, has lacked coherence, continuity, and visibility. Texts on the "psychology of religion" have generally omitted any reference to the use of psychological approaches to Scripture (Kille 1992; Miell 1990). David Wulff notes that the field of psychology of religion is "hopelessly diffuse," and his comment is equally apt regarding psychology and the Bible:

> Psychologists, psychiatrists, anthropologists, historians of religion, theologians, and religious educators, among others, bring with them widely varying backgrounds, assumptions, and interests. Furthermore . . . the typical contributor makes but a single, incidental incursion into the field, commonly without a guiding theory or hypothesis. Rarely . . . do contributors demonstrate familiarity with more than a single area of research. (Wulff 1985:23–24)

PSYCHOLOGICAL CRITICISM: DEFINITION

Amid this ferment, psychological criticism is emerging as a branch of biblical studies in its own right. Not only have psychologists, theologians, and biblical scholars attended specifically to psychological issues in biblical interpretation, but biblical scholars from such diverse approaches as feminist, ideological, deconstructionist, reader-response, and structuralist criticism have adopted theories and assumptions from psychology. The fact that "Psychology and Biblical Studies" was established as a program unit within the Society for Biblical Literature in 1991 shows the new importance of psychological study within biblical studies.

This interest brings with it renewed effort to define the field as practitioners seek to establish, legitimate, and clarify the place and role of psychological criticism within biblical studies. Different writers have used differing names for their efforts. G. Stanley Hall and F. C. Grant proposed "psychological criticism." Gerd Theissen described his work as "psychological exegesis," or "a hermeneutically oriented psychology of religion" (1987). Others have suggested "psychoanalytic reading of the Bible," "psychological hermeneutics," or "psychological or psychoanalytic approach." All of these terms tend to confine the scope of the approach, either by limiting it to one aspect of biblical interpretation such as exegesis or hermeneutics, or to one category of psychological theory such as psychoanalysis. For our purposes here we shall use "psychological biblical criticism," a term that suggests we are speaking about the intersections of three fields: psychology, the Bible, and the tradition of rigorous, critical reading of the biblical text (Rollins 1999).

One can legitimately argue that *all* critical methods have psychological dimensions, as all involve the human psyche in perception, cognition, and interpretation, but not all methods are properly named "psychological criticism." Can we yet speak of a discipline of "psychological criticism"? What characterizes the approach, and how is it distinct from other methods that might share its concerns?

In his recent book, *Soul and Psyche*, Wayne Rollins, who has done more to re-establish psychological criticism within contemporary biblical studies than any other individual, offers this encompassing definition of psychological biblical criticism:

> The goal of a psychological-critical approach is to examine texts, their origination, authorship, modes of expression, their construction, transmission, translation, reading, interpretation, their transposition into kindred and alien art forms, and the history of their personal and cultural effect, as expressions of the structure, processes, and habits of the human psyche, both in individual and collective manifestations, past and present. (Rollins 1999:77–78)

Rollins's effort was one of the first attempts to identify and categorize the current state of the field as it emerges. His definition is broad, perhaps as broad as our initial definition of psychology as the study of behavior. Since "origination, authorship . . . expression . . . construction, transmission, translation, reading, interpretation," and so on are all human behaviors, they all legitimately fall under the potential concern of psychology. To give more form and definition to the field, Rollins set forth an agenda for psychological criticism that comprises six potential areas of investigation: the history of biblical psychology, development of models for psychological criticism, exegesis, hermeneutics, psychological description of biblical religious phenomena, and the history of the effects of the biblical text on its readers. Psychological biblical criticism encompasses all of these dimensions of the text and human interactions with it.

2
Psychological Biblical Criticism: Questions, History, and Methods

Although psychology and biblical interpretation are no strangers to each other, the relationship between the two has been problematic for a number of reasons. This is perhaps not surprising, given that, in a sense, psychology and theology are competing worldviews, each with its own answers to questions of human life, purpose, and salvation or wholeness (Vitz 1985). Despite having historical roots in theology, contemporary psychology as a social science traces its origins to Wilhelm Wundt's foundation of a school for experimental psychology at Leipzig in 1879. The effect of Wundt's "founding" of modern psychology was to wrest the discipline from its roots in philosophy and theology and replant it in the soil of rationalist, positivist science. "It was the stabilization of a meaning of a word . . . and an arrogation of that 'new' meaning to sovereign status over all prior usages. . . . Henceforward, the core meaning of 'psychology' would be dominated by the adjectives scientific and experimental" (Koch and Leary 1992:8).

Many of the key figures in psychology emerged from highly religious backgrounds or held great concern for religious issues, notably Freud, Jung, and Adler, as well as William James, G. Stanley Hall, Carl Rogers, Erich Fromm, Rollo May, Karl Menninger, and Elisabeth Kübler-Ross. Early psychologists (or other scholars borrowing psychological theories) were not averse to applying their newly developed perspectives to interpretations of the biblical text. Unfortunately, these efforts earned the scorn (often justified) of other interpreters. Psychology itself was as yet an undeveloped discipline and its theories and methodologies were often clumsy and reductionist. At the same time, antagonisms between psychology and theology further complicated their interaction. Perhaps trying to distance themselves from the philosophical and theological origins of their discipline and to assert the positivist, materialist "science" of psychology, many psychologists were extremely hostile to religion, seeing it as illusive at best and pathological at worst. Psychologists remain the least religious of all scientists, according to several recent studies. Their heavy-handed efforts to interpret Scripture were met with hostility on the part of biblical scholars, who were skeptical of this new orientation and its claims.

Some early psychological interpreters of Scripture attempted almost gleefully to describe biblical figures like the prophets, Paul, and Jesus in pathological terms. Without articulating or reflecting critically on their psychological (and textual) models and assumptions, they accepted the biblical text as reliably historical and focused on the unusual: "the personality of Job, the consciousness of Jesus, the conversion of Paul, as (essentially abnormal) phenomena requiring (and legitimating) ad hoc psychoanalytic explanations" (Miell 1990:571).

Other attempts to explain Jesus as an ecstatic, an epileptic, a "paranoiac," and "a case of nerves" were adamantly rejected (Bundy 1922). Albert Schweitzer's thesis for the M.D. degree at Strasbourg University in 1913 brought the same scholarly attention that he had previously employed in his critique *The Quest for the Historical Jesus* to bear on these psychological portraits. The painters of psychopathological portraits of Jesus were guilty of ignoring the historical development and context of the gospel writings and had "constructed pictures of sickness which are themselves artifacts and which, moreover, cannot be made to conform exactly with the clinical forms of sickness diagnosed by the authors" (1948:75).

Although biblical scholars never took such pathological portraits of Jesus and other figures very seriously, reaction to such readings was sufficiently strong to make any psychological interpretation of the Bible suspect. Nor was the early enthusiasm of psychologists to continue. Annual reviews of the psychology of religion, which had been published in the *Psychological Bulletin*, ceased in 1928. Only in the 1960s was there a revival marked by the founding of the Society for the Scientific Study of Religion and the Christian Association for Psychological Studies. The Catholic Psychological Association began meeting jointly with the American Psychological Association, which led eventually to the creation for the first time of a division of the APA for "Psychologists Interested in Religious Issues"

(Division 36) in 1975. A handful of psychologists continued to work with biblical texts, but mainstream biblical scholars routinely dismissed works on the psychology of the Bible for the better part of the twentieth century. The dominant attitude is summed up in the comment by Gerd Theissen that "[e]very exegete has learned that psychological exegesis is bad exegesis" and Robin Scroggs's report of a scholar's admonition that "[Rudolf] Bultmann taught us years ago to be suspicious of psychology" (Theissen 1987:1; Scroggs 1982:335).

CHANGING ATTITUDES

Yet, as Scroggs, Theissen, and others have shown, psychological criticism is enjoying new respectability within biblical studies. What has brought about this change in attitude? Several key factors have each had a part in bringing new vitality to psychological criticism: the development and maturing of psychological theory and methods, the "psychologization" of Western culture, and the decline of the dominance of the historical-critical method within biblical studies.

Development of Psychological Theory

Psychology has undergone profound changes since Wundt's time. The initial optimism that psychology could become a unified scientific field on the order of the natural sciences has failed to become a reality. In the past century psychology has expanded immensely into an impressive array of subdisciplines (including sensory processes and perception, learning theory, cognition, development, physiology, and psychotherapy) and often contradictory and competing schools of thought (such as functionalism, Gestalt psychology, behaviorism, depth psychology, phenomenology, and "third force"). While these groups occasionally interact with each other, bitter disputes over the object and methodology of research often characterize such encounters. Not even the definition of psychology itself has found common agreement. As of 1992, there were no fewer than forty-two specialized divisions within the American Psychological Association, and each division itself contains many subgroups whose members think and act differently.

Two significant directions of development within psychology bear on the significance of psychological criticism for biblical studies: a movement away from an earlier exclusive focus on the individual toward more interactive and relational theories, and the metatheoretical observation that psychology (as in all sciences) is itself a *hermeneutical* system, a system of interpretation.

Since the Bible is not purely a historical account of individual personalities but is rather a text that has undergone literary transformations, editing, and theological transformations, a naive application of personalized psychology to biblical figures is highly problematic. Attention to psychosocial interactions, the role of communities and traditions in shaping perceptions and worldviews, and especially to the relationship of the contemporary reader to the text offer much more fruitful avenues of inquiry.

Second, recognition of the hermeneutical dimensions of psychological theory serves to bring the disciplines of psychology and biblical interpretation onto common ground. The thesis that scientific advances come primarily through "paradigm shifts," that is, changing frameworks of interpretation, has challenged the positivist view of progressive, "objective" science. Choices of phenomena to study, the methods of observation, and the interpretation of data all reflect theoretical preconceptions. Furthermore, psychology has often depended on metaphorical language to describe human behavior. Depth psychologies in particular appear as hermeneutical strategies. Seen in this light, a multiplicity of psychological theories appears not so much as a failure of scientific method, but as a conflict of interpretations, to use Paul Ricoeur's phrase. Psychological events have more than one cause and their meaning is taken from a multitude of interrelationships with context, culture, and experience, which presents many opportunities for interpretation. Depending on their choice of data, their aims (psychological or other), and even their own personalities, language capabilities, and biases, theorists will organize and value behaviors in differing ways and develop different concepts and vocabularies to express their findings.

The hermeneutical dimension of all science is heightened by the unique challenge that "in psychology, the means by which you study the psyche is the psyche itself . . . the observer is the observed. The psyche is not only the object, but also the subject of our science" (Jung 1976:¶277). Psychology is inextricably intertwined with the hermeneutical dimensions of the subject, the object, and the relationship between the two.

Since psychological theories represent competing hermeneutical approaches, how can or should they relate to one another and to the practice of biblical hermeneutics in particular? Is there, for example, a mediating position between behaviorism, which confines itself to observation of overt behavior, and depth psychology with its concern for unconscious motivations? Or, within depth psychology, can there be a meeting place between Freud's distorting personal unconscious and Jung's unitive collective unconscious? One possibility would be to abandon any effort at mediation and to consider each theory as an independent "community of interpretation" à la Stanley Fish. Paul Feyerabend has proposed just such a "theoretical pluralism" of mutually inconsistent theories. For the most part, psychology in general, and psychological approaches to the Bible in particular, have operated under such a model. Proponents of one approach or another have proceeded in splendid isolation from each other, ignorant of other perspectives or rejecting them outright.

A more productive possibility would be a methodological pluralism in which varying theories would enter into the "conflict of interpretations," each bringing its own perspective but open to insights from the others. Within such a plurality must be the recognition that no one method will be sufficient to illuminate all aspects of a text, and that one cannot assess one method in the terms of another.

Ricoeur's important study on the impact of Freudian theory on hermeneutics has established the "hermeneutic of suspicion" as a basic concept in contemporary hermeneutical theory (1970). Under the influence of psychoanalytic theory, interpreters are no longer willing to accept a text at face value. Rather, Freud (with Marx and Nietzsche) taught us "to doubt consciousness." The task now is not only to explicate conscious meaning but to decipher expressions of hidden levels of meaning. This insight has opened the way for contemporary biblical interpretations from feminist and Marxist positions, for example.

Peter Homans's exploration of the interrelation of psychology and hermeneutics has led him to observe that contemporary hermeneutical theory has begun to incorporate psychological insights, both implicitly and explicitly. The key issues of hermeneutics—the subjectivity of the interpreter, the nature of the thing being interpreted, and the means of mediating between the two—all have psychological implications. While Freudian analysis has proved most adaptable and popular within hermeneutics, Homans suggests that structuralist perspectives (by which he means the theories of Piaget, Kohlberg, and Loevinger), which detail the development of cognitive and moral development, may prove more fruitful for addressing hermeneutical issues.

Jung developed his own characteristic hermeneutical methods, with implications for interpretation. Homans describes Jung's "psychological hermeneutic" as a dynamic and subjective approach that brings together the realms of hermeneutics and psychology through interpretation of the religious image. Jung first seeks the religious image or symbol beneath doctrine in order to prepare the way for a new appropriation of the symbol as a living religious experience. Wayne Rollins has explored in depth the implications of Jung's theory for biblical interpretation. The Bible, as with all religious texts, has been shaped not only by sociological and historical forces but by the structures of human personality, both conscious and unconscious. Jung's theory offers a unique resource for dealing with biblical phenomena: symbols, archetypal images, myths, dreams, personalities, religious experience, pathogenic and therapeutic elements, and the interrelationship of the reader and text (Rollins 1983).

Psychology and Contemporary Culture

A second factor affecting psychological criticism stems from the impact that psychology has had on twentieth-century Western culture. Phrases such as "Freudian slip," "Oedipus complex," the "unconscious," "projection," and "free association," once the specialized vocabulary of psychologists, have now become a part of daily conversation and the stuff of literature, movies, and television. The "self-help" shelves in many bookstores are packed with volumes that promise to help us understand ourselves and others better. Cartoonists and television writers presume that the audience will understand the character on the couch, or the bearded analyst with the German accent. Newspaper reporters and columnists speculate on possible "unconscious" motivations for actions reported in the news, and public courtroom dramas play out issues of mental states and responsibility. We are confronted daily with the shared understanding that our behavior is molded by factors that are hidden to our conscious minds. Peter Homans has observed how psychoanalytic ideas in particular have become in America "a guiding set of ideas woven into the fabric of its institutional life," shaping a new social being that he denotes as "psychological [hu]man" (1979). However simplistic their understanding might be, contemporary readers of the Bible intuitively know that it has something to say about the human psyche. Simply reading psychological theory into the Bible is anachronistic, at the very least. The authors and compilers of the text did not inhabit the world of the "psychological human." They did not use the distinctly modern categories of psychological language or thought. They did, however, amply describe human behavior: emotion, motivation, will, and choice. Modern biblical scholars, both influenced by and seeking to communicate intelligibly to a "psychologized" culture, are well served by gaining some familiarity with psychological categories.

Shifts within Biblical Studies

The third factor leading to greater openness to psychological criticism reflects the decline of the dominance of historical-critical methods within biblical studies and the proliferation of new methods and perspectives. In recent years there has been a growing recognition that historical-critical methods, while holding an essential place among the tools of biblical criticism, cannot serve as the only way to approach the text. New methods have come into acceptance and older methods have been recovered. Historical criticism is now just one of a wide range of methods for biblical study, taking its place alongside structuralist, linguistic, literary, sociological, reader-oriented, ideological, and feminist approaches, to name just a few.

Alongside, and sometimes in concert with, these new methods, psychological criticism enjoys renewed acceptance. Within the historical, referential paradigm, psychology had limited value. Biblical materials offer scant data for analysis of historical persons or of the authors of the texts, and transmission and redaction have tremendously complicated what data does exist. Many psychological "interpretations" of the Bible have suffered by attempting such "historical psychoanalysis," often fatally flawed by ignorance or disregard for historical context and/or transmission. Psychology may, however, have much to offer for explaining psychological dynamics of the texts and how they affect the reader.

MAPPING THE FIELD

Clearly, there are many possible intersections of the concerns of psychology with the phenomena of the biblical text and its interpretation. As we noted above, each individual who approaches the text with an eye sensitive to psychological phenomena will identify different aspects and valences of the text. Can we begin to identify and group issues and approaches to better understand the range and purposes of psychological biblical criticism?

As mentioned above, Rollins has suggested an "agenda" for the field that outlines six fundamental areas of concern: the history of biblical psychology, development of models for psychological criticism, exegesis, hermeneutics, psychological description of biblical religious phenomena, and the history of the effects of the biblical text on readers and communities of readers.

Biblical Psychology

One significant task is to recover and re-evaluate the long history of biblical psychology. Franz Delitzsch in the mid-1800s declared biblical psychology to be "one of the oldest sciences of the church" and traced its history from roots in the early church fathers through Augustine and Reformation scholars to the more systematic and "scientific" works of the late eighteenth and early nineteenth centuries. From Tertullian's *De Anima* ("Concerning the Soul") and Augustine's writings on the soul to Philip Melanchton's coinage of the term *psychology* to Delitzsch's own *A System of Biblical Psychology* and M. Scott Fletcher's *A Psychology of the New Testament,* there is a rich body of work which seeks both to describe the nature of the human psyche/soul as presented in the biblical texts and to put forth guidelines for "soul-healthy" living. Rollins explores these works in depth in the first chapter of *Soul and Psyche* (1999).

Together with the task of recovering "biblical psychology" there is a challenge to identify how biblical concepts of human behavior influenced psychological theorists. Not only did many key thinkers in psychology come from overtly Christian or Jewish backgrounds, they came also out of Western culture, which has been as thoroughly influenced by the sacred writings of the Bible as it has come to be shaped by psychological perspectives. What role, conscious or unconscious, did biblical psychology play in the formation of this new science?

Finally, there is a challenge to take seriously the tension that often exists between modern psychological and biblical understandings of humanity. Even as we ask what psychology may contribute to biblical studies, we must ask what the Bible may have to say to psychology. It is not adequate for the world of the Bible and the world of psychology to operate as if the other did not exist. Nor is it appropriate to reduce either one to the other. Rather, it is in serious dialogue between the two fields that creative engagement can occur.

Theoretical Foundations

Rollins's second proposition calls for an effort to elaborate a theoretical basis for psychological criticism. In part, the failure of psychological criticism to achieve wider recognition and acceptance has been due to a lack of coherent canons for such study. Critics have failed to reflect carefully on their methods, have applied psychological theories indiscriminately, and have not considered the interrelationship of psychological criticism and other methods of biblical criticism. Nor have they been careful about issues that are raised by cultural distance and the hazards of arbitrarily applying modern psychological categories to texts from the ancient world.

Some of the past sins of psychological criticism may well be attributed to the effort to fit into the dominant historical-critical model and to the relative newness of psychology itself. In recent years, increasing sophistication within psychology and the development of models for applying social science to biblical interpretation have served to mitigate some of the earlier shortcomings. Still, there is a need to be aware of the potential distortions associated with reductionism, "psychologism," and cultural distance.

While such a conscious formulation of a theoretical base for psychological criticism is a necessary task for each critic, it is not likely that such efforts will issue in any kind of unanimous opinion, given the complexity and diversity within both psychology and biblical studies. Gerd Theissen, in *Psychological Aspects of Pauline Theology* (1987), attempts a unified synthesis of several theories that proves possible only by neglecting key pieces of each theory. Nevertheless, if psychological biblical criticism is to move beyond its fragmentary and disconnected history, much work must be done on identifying methodological concerns, comparing the relative usefulness of varying methods, and encouraging ongoing dialogue among those using the approach.

Exegesis

Biblical exegesis has sometimes been narrowly defined as historical investigation into the original historical context and authorial intention of the text. To that end, exegesis has been based on examination of the historical, linguistic, social, and literary factors. Psychological exegesis, Rollins argues, calls attention to an additional element that is equally a part of any context—human psychology. Both conscious and unconscious factors in the author, community, and the historical situation shape the "selection, formulation, organization, and rhetorical orientation of the textual materials." Rollins is quite correct in his assertion that the most significant contribution of psychological criticism to biblical studies lies in its attention to this universal, yet commonly overlooked, dimension of the text.

One does not gain access to these psychic dimensions easily, and indeed, some have questioned whether it is even possible. However, three elements of the biblical text provide potential starting points: symbols and archetypal images, psychodynamic factors represented in narrative and discourse, and depictions of biblical personalities.

First, psychological analysis of biblical images and symbols, when undertaken with careful attention to cultural contexts, can highlight archetypal commonalities and psychic valences of such images as the tree of life or the primordial garden. Such an investigation assumes, as Rollins rightly points out, a continuity of psychological makeup between the ancient writers and the modern interpreter. All biblical exegesis, however, rests on similar assumptions of continuity, at least to the extent that the modern interpreter can comprehend the ancient text and draw meaning from it. The effort to illuminate the meaning of symbols by means of comparison to other ancient Near Eastern cultures and representations is an accepted exegetical method (see Rashkow 2000). Such comparisons might further provide data to prove a commonality of meaning founded in common human psychic processes.

Second, one can examine the psychodynamics of biblical texts—that is, the way the texts reflect established psychological models of the development, expression, and interrelationships of human cognition and behavior. Rollins mentions such patterns as "repression, denial, sublimation, projection, regression, displacement, transference and reaction formation" (1999:44). One must apply psychological models with great care, since failing to recognize historical or literary factors may lead to simply imposing the theory on the text and forcing it to fit the exegete's pet perceptions.

Third, regarding the psychological analysis of biblical personalities it is essential to recognize the limitations of the biblical text with regard to psychological contents. The authors and compilers of the text did not use psychological language, nor did they intend to write case histories or personal journals. Although certain aspects of biblical terminology can be translated into psychological terms by analogy, the "psychological human" is a distinctly modern phenomenon.

Despite the liveliness of biblical personalities such as the prophets, patriarchs, and matriarchs, and the almost irresistible urge to psychoanalyze them, one must keep in mind that layers of transmission, tradition, and literary development have placed us at a great distance from the living persons (if, indeed, some of them even were historical persons). What we know of the biblical world is only a small piece of the totality of the cultures, and what we find in the Bible is a smaller sample yet. Few contemporary therapists would venture a diagnosis of a patient from such partial and modified evidence.

"Historical psychoanalysis" of Bible characters has been a popular and highly abused psychological approach in the past, rightfully deserving the scorn it has received. Rollins's assertion that such efforts still offer significant potential requires a caveat. Recognizing that true psychoanalysis is impossible is essential, given that the analysand is not present and that literary composition, convention, and transmission have shaped biblical personages beyond personality factors. On the other hand, psychological literary critics have long appreciated that literary characters do indeed have a "life of their own." Part of the power of literature depends on constructed characters that accurately reflect human experience and behavior. Exercised with great caution to avoid the historical and literary naïveté of earlier efforts, psychological criticism can clarify and highlight psychodynamic factors exhibited by and through biblical figures.

Hermeneutics

Hermeneutics is potentially even more fruitful for psychological criticism in that it can examine the interaction of a modern reader with the text in the construction of meaning. We have already mentioned that psychological theories themselves function as hermeneutical frameworks. The interaction of reader and text is not only evident in living readers, whose interpretations and personalities can be observed directly, but is also shown in the long history of biblical interpretation as exegesis and exposition reveal how the text has affected readers.

Contemporary structuralist, ideological, and reader-response strategies of biblical criticism have often alluded to psychological theory in identifying how language functions in the creation of worldviews and interpretive frameworks. Psychological criticism simply makes explicit the specifically psychological dimensions, implicit in such analyses, of the complex interactions of presuppositions, social interaction, experience, and language that contribute to the meaning of a text. Psychologically informed hermeneutics will not overlook the role that the biblical text can play in engaging the heart, soul, mind, and will of the reader.

Theissen proposed some conscious presuppositions that provide a theoretical foundation for what he calls "hermeneutically oriented psychology." Human experience and behavior are mediated by interpretation, are historically conditioned, marked by content and can be objectified in texts and form a unified whole. Since the objectifications of experience are interpreted and codified in texts, and are to some extent analogous to modern consciousness, making meaningful connections between the ancient text and the modern reader is possible (1987:2–3).

Two aspects of the interaction of reader and text are of particular significance for psychological criticism: that texts are inherently expressive of multiple meanings and that the personality of the interpreter affects interpretation. Ricoeur has elaborated on what he calls "the surplus of meaning" and the projection of the "world in front of the text." Reader-response critics such as Wolfgang Iser and Umberto Eco also have described the reader's process of moving through a text, anticipating what will come next and integrating each new expression into a unified sense of the "meaning" of the text. Most reader-response analyses attend only to conscious choices in interpretation; however, psychological criticism will also consider unconscious associations by author and reader as factors in reading and understanding.

Interpreters' personalities or "psychological types" also affect interpretation. Ever since Schleiermacher, hermeneutical theory has noted the importance of the reader's presuppositions. Each interpreter approaches the text with his or her own theories, concepts, context, and attitudes. The process of reading subsequently is shaped by and, in turn, reshapes those pre-interpretations. This process is what has come to be known as the "hermeneutic circle." More than a simple back-and-forth between interpreter and text, the process is more of a "spiral" of developing understanding. A psychologically informed hermeneutics will alert us to yet another dimension of presuppositions—those that arise out of the personality and unconscious of the interpreter. Jung proposed a model of four basic personality types, noting differing ways individuals experienced and organized their worlds. Not only interpretive choices, but the very choices of theory and method themselves may in part reflect the personality of the interpreter (Johnson 1983). A study of college students found a high correlation between personality scores on the Meyers-Briggs Type Indicator test (based on Jungian types) and the individual's preferred interpretations of Bible passages (Bassett, Mathewson, and Galitis 1993).

An interpreter's affinity for (or rejection of) historical, sociological, or structural methods may also be related to personality structures. Certainly, personality is not the sole factor—history, geography, teachers, and environment all play a part—but personality cannot be ignored as an influence.

On a deeper level, the interpreter's own unconscious may also affect interpretation. In an overlooked article in 1950, W. Oates noted that a pastoral counselor could use the Bible as a diagnostic tool, since "the Bible is a mirror into which a person projects his own concept of himself, and which in turn reflects it back with accuracy" (1950:43). Although Oates was primarily concerned with pathological interpretations, there is no doubt that any reading of the Bible will say something about the interpreter as well as the text. T. Reik noted that many well-respected contemporary biblical scholars of his day had suggested emendations of the Masoretic text of Gen 26:7, softening what Reik takes to be a clear reference to Isaac's incestuous attraction to his mother. By suggesting that the text refers instead to his feelings for his father, these exegetes are engaging in rationalization by reacting to their own unconscious rejection of the unthinkable.

One can approach these unconscious dimensions of the interaction of reader and text through techniques that have developed within psychotherapy. Thus the Freudian strategy of free association and the Jungian practices of amplification and active imagination allow unconscious connections to be made visible. Centuries of midrash, art, music, drama, preaching, and teaching based upon the Bible serve as a resource for recognizing the diversity and richness of human associations with the images, symbols, and narratives it presents.

The psychotherapeutic phenomenon of countertransference may offer a further route for exploration of unconscious dimensions in reading the text.

Countertransference occurs in psychotherapy when a therapist develops an affective response toward a patient, involving the therapist's projection of his or her own unconscious content onto the patient. An important aspect of therapy is the therapist's ability to recognize and acknowledge countertransference. While attempts to treat a text as though it were a patient (or the symptoms of the author) have been justly criticized, the fact that a text can stir up response in the reader is undeniable. Literary critic Arthur Marotti contends that countertransference issues do arise in the experience of literature and, in fact, are vital for understanding any work of art. He quotes psychoanalytic anthropologist George Devereaux to say that if a reader "ignores these responses—that is, resists them—he will develop a 'pseudo-methodology' since his rational strategies will then be as much an unconscious defense against inner disruption as a cognitively suitable reaction to the outside world" (1978:473). Murray Stein describes Jung's *Answer to Job*, Jung's only extended work of biblical interpretation, as an expression of Jung's own countertransference reaction to Christianity (1985:162–63).

Religious Phenomena

As a religious text, the Bible describes and illustrates an array of religious experiences, both personal and communal. Psychological description and analysis of these biblical religious phenomena would constitute Rollins's fifth area of study. In conjunction with other social sciences and literary criticisms, psychological critics would examine conventional religious experience and practice as well as unusual or "paranormal" religious experiences. From the everyday practice of prayer, religious ritual, and the social psychology of religious communities to the extraordinary practice of glossolalia, ecstatic activity, and demon possession, the whole range of religious behavior described and prescribed within biblical texts, together with the role the texts play in contemporary religious experience, provides a rich resource for reflection. Biblical accounts of dreams, visions, prophetic activity, or mystical experiences can be explored with due respect for the limits imposed by historical and literary distance. Rituals such as sacrifice, the Eucharist, baptism, and footwashing each have their inner impact on readers and participants. Finally, psychospiritual, experiential phenomena—sin, guilt, grace, forgiveness, salvation, redemption, millennial and apocalyptic thinking, conversion, and rebirth—all have psychological dimensions.

History of Biblical Effects

The final task for psychological criticism in Rollins's view is to trace the history of how the Bible has shaped human consciousness and cognition for good or ill. Even as traditional biblical study has been so concerned with the meaning and impact of the text and its antecedents on the people of its historical era, this "history of biblical effects" would examine the psychospiritual impact of the Bible on both individuals and communities over time, as it has given rise both to therapeutic and pathogenic responses. Pastors and pastoral counselors have long understood that the Bible can be used therapeutically in counseling situations, as articles in *Pastoral Counseling*, the *Journal of Psychology and Christianity*, the *Journal of Psychology and Judaism*, and the *Journal of Psychology and Theology* amply demonstrate. Work has also been done on the ways in which biblical texts have both given rise to, and are used to justify, such pathological expressions as racism, anti-Semitism, and spousal and child abuse.

RELATIONSHIP TO OTHER METHODS OF BIBLICAL CRITICISM

Although we have given only a brief treatment to each of these possible dimensions of psychological biblical criticism, it is clearly evident that no single methodology can deal with such varied and diverse materials. Not only because of the diversity of issues to be considered, but because the very diversity of psychology as a discipline precludes any single approach. Cognitive psychologists, behaviorists, and depth psychologists will identify and describe widely differing aspects of each issue. Even among the broad groupings of theories there will be disagreement—Freudians will not see what Jungians find unmistakable, and vice versa.

Within biblical studies we might locate psychological criticism in relation to two widely acknowledged current approaches: feminist criticism and sociological criticism. Psychological criticism is akin to feminist biblical criticism in that it is not so much a method (or even a cluster of methods) as it is a *way of reading*. Feminist criticism is sensitive to historical, contextual, and ideological factors that affect women. In so doing, it may draw upon other disciplines of criticism, theology, and hermeneutics, and address different aspects of the text, but the framework for reading is always women's experience. Similarly, psychological hermeneutics is a way of reading that is critically sensitive to the psychological interactions in and beyond the text. It is significant that many feminist biblical scholars such as Mieke Bal, Julia Kristeva, Mary Ann Tolbert, and Ilona Rashkow draw explicitly upon psychological theory.

On the other hand, sociological criticism *is* a method, one that draws upon models of another social science. Sociology is closely related to psychology in that it concentrates on group behavior, while psychology tends to focus on the individual. Corporate behavior is generally more identifiable and homogeneous than individual behavior, and thus is somewhat more amenable to more systematic and methodological treatment. The boundaries between more socially informed psychology and sociology overlap in dealing with the construction of symbolic worlds, concepts of "dyadic" personality, and deviance theory. It is no mere coincidence that one of the most painstakingly methodological efforts at psychological exegesis has been done by Gerd Theissen, who is well known for his sociological studies of first-century Christianity.

When drawing upon psychological theory in relation to texts, psychological criticism will encounter many of the same methodological issues raised by scholars using models from other social sciences such as sociology. Among these issues are questions of the *reliability* of the text (how convention, transmission, etc., have altered primary information); *competence with the models* of the discipline of reference (knowing their strengths and limitations); and *validity* (whether a twentieth-century model is, in fact, appropriate to the text and at what level of generalization). Some of the data and methods of sociological analysis will be shared by psychology. Insights may be built on inferences from events, social norms, and symbolic systems; these may be illuminated by comparison to contemporary culture or by analogy to comparable phenomena, including the modern.

Psychological analysis must also deal with the temptation to psychologism, that is, reducing every dimension of the text to fit a psychological theory or perspective. Even Freud noted that psychological phenomena are "overdetermined," that is, they arise out of the interaction of many causes, not just one. While psychologism is a legitimate concern for psychological criticism, the term has often been used by others to dismiss any effort to make explicit the psychological dynamics of the text. Psychological criticism also finds much common ground with literary, reader-response, and ideological approaches. Psychological criticism is firmly established as a subdiscipline of contemporary literary theory. Interpretive strategies used in psychological literary criticism cannot be imported uncritically to biblical studies due to the differences between ancient and contemporary literature, but when used with discrimination can suggest fruitful avenues of inquiry. Reader-response and ideological criticism both move from analysis of how texts "work" to examination of what they work upon: the individual reader (reader-response) and the reader in social context or world-view (ideological). Close observation of the interaction of a reader and the text, on what the reader brings to reading, and how the process of reading affects the reader can illuminate significant psychic factors. We have also noted the significant influence of Freud in the development of a hermeneutic of suspicion that undergirds ideological criticism, and the similarities between psychological criticism and one form of ideological criticism: feminist reading. Ideological criticisms seek to unmask the ways in which a text invites or constrains readers to adopt particular perspectives and how those constructed worldviews shape communities, individuals, and other texts. Such analysis touches on questions of cognition, perceptual frameworks, and behavior—all fruitful dimensions for psychological insight.

It is worthwhile to note that all of the methods of biblical criticism mentioned above have emerged within the latter part of the twentieth century as historical-critical methods were called into question. Psychoanalytic criticism is included in *The Postmodern Bible,* together with reader-response, structuralist, poststructuralist, rhetorical, feminist, womanist, and ideological criticisms, as a method which offers new possibilities for biblical study (Aichele et al. 1995). At its best, psychological criticism will use all the available interpretive tools—linguistic, structural, stylistic, historical, and sociological—adding an informed sensitivity to the psychodynamics of human interaction, communication, and symbolization. A multidisciplinary approach serves as a hedge against psychologism, which is the reduction of all phenomena to psychological categories. Complexities of the text itself, its origins, and its effects can no more be exhausted by psychology than they can be by history, social forces, politics, theology, or any other discipline.

THREE DIMENSIONS OF TEXT

Extending Ricoeur's concept of the "world in front of the text," Sandra Schneiders suggests a helpful three-dimensional model for understanding the different aspects of texts and their interpretations. In each dimension, or "world," the focus of study is slightly different, and the appropriate interpretive tools differ as well. We can speak usefully of the world *behind* the text—the historical referents, the authors, and the world in which the Bible was shaped. There is the world *of* the text—structures of narrative, characterization, and language. And there is the world *in front of* the text—the "potential horizons of meaning which may be actualized in different ways" (Ricoeur 1976:78). Genuine contributions of psychological interpretations have often been muted or distorted by confusion among these levels (Schneiders 1991).

The World behind the Text

For Romantic hermeneutics (as in Schleiermacher), a text meant what the author intended it to mean. From this perspective, the task of the interpreter would be to understand as much as possible about the background, attitudes, culture, and logic of the author. Much of the work of traditional historical-critical biblical study is based on this position. Textual, source, form, and redaction criticism attempt to recover the original, or earlier form, of the texts. Linguistic studies of phonology, lexicology, grammar, and syntax seek to understand how the original languages were used and what they might have meant to the original author and the original audience. Studies of the history and culture of the text's original setting provide potential insight into the thought patterns and modes of expression that may have shaped the author's intentions.

Historical and sociological studies also illuminate the world behind the text by filling out what Ricoeur calls the "reference" of a text, in contrast to its "sense." The sense of a text is "what" it says; the reference is the "about what," such as description, allusion, and truth claims. Investigation of geographical settings, customs and rituals, social organization, daily life, and historical events can create better understanding of references within our texts.

Perhaps due to the dominance of historical-critical methods, early interpreters often attempted to use psychology as a tool for "historical" investigation by analyzing the writers and personalities within the Scriptures.

Many psychological approaches, especially of the Freudian school, focused on analyzing the psyche of the author behind the text, explicating the apostle Paul's internal struggles or the "paranoid schizophrenia" of the author of Revelation. Some attempted to reconstruct the "self-consciousness" of Jesus or to explore the phenomenology of demon possession or ecstatic charismatic gifts. But, as we have seen, the Bible usually provides inadequate information for such investigations. An appreciation for the way the text is an artifact of a historical and literary process and not simply a transparent report of individual thoughts or emotions can serve as a corrective to psychologism. However, recovering personalities behind the text is not entirely impossible. One significant recent effort to do just that is David Halperin's *Seeking Ezekiel*. Halperin meticulously notes textual, linguistic, and thematic problems long familiar to biblical critics and demonstrates that an appreciation for psychological dynamics may, in fact, offer some solutions to those problems (1993).

For the most part, though, psychology may best serve in the world behind the text as yet one more way to illuminate the context and references of ancient documents. It most certainly can play a descriptive role in seeking to illuminate certain scriptural phenomena (such as glossolalia) by analogy to the modern world, in exploring the dynamics of language and memory in the transmission of oral tradition, or in pointing out developmental issues reflected in the texts.

A recent new direction in biblical criticism has reshaped the question of authorial intention. Formerly, the emphasis of criticism has been on texts as language. But communication is not only language; it is also action, that is, behavior. Speech-act theory analyzes the ability of language to influence actions, change perspectives, offer hope, or bring healing. From this perspective, authorial intent is not defined in terms of the individual psychology of the author as a person but as the directedness of the speech acts expressed in the text. Certainly the hearing, understanding, and responding to speech or text all involve psychological processes of cognition, valuation, and intention and would be appropriate directions for analysis.

The World of the Text

Analysis of biblical figures and of the dynamics of relationships in the Bible belongs more properly to the narrative world *of* the text. As in literary criticism, psychologically informed criticism can describe the qualities of a character as he or she is presented in the text, but must take care neither to presume that those characterizations are historical nor to go beyond the text by filling in details that are suggested more by the interpreter's chosen theory than by the text itself. This filling in often proves to be a particular hazard of psychological readings. Phrases such as "it is possible/likely that . . . ," "we may assume that . . . ," "this may indicate that . . . ," "this is reminiscent of . . . ," and "this is no more than . . . " usually are markers of aspects of a theory being imported into a text. As Dominique Stein aptly puts it, "Many 'psycho-analytic' readings . . . come down to being an application (in the sense in which we say we *apply* a dressing) of a pre-established grill familiar to the author on—not to—a text which serves more as a proof than as object of study" (1980:27). On the other hand, filling in can be a legitimate aspect of amplification of the text, but as such belongs properly to the world *in front of* the text and the reader's interaction with it (see below).

Recent literary approaches to Scripture have suggested that more insight into character and motivation is revealed than was previously thought. Unlike modern novels, which offer explicit descriptions of the thoughts and consciousness of characters, biblical characterization depends on narrative and especially speech to portray personality, as Alter has so clearly demonstrated (1981; 1992). Yael Feldman has suggested that the "gap filling" readings used by Alter and Meier Sternberg are, in effect, Freudian interpretive strategies, although without Freudian analysis (1989). Proper understanding of such portrayals, however, requires close reading of the text and awareness of the context and literary conventions of the writings.

Deconstructive readings of texts represent a radicalization of Saussure's linguistics. Taking its point of departure from Saussure's assertion that the relationship of a sign and its referent is only arbitrary, deconstructionism asserts that in the last analysis, texts do not have any reference outside their own frame. The indeterminate signs of the text only point to other signs, which in turn are likewise indeterminate. Reading then becomes

> not the reactualization of a meaning that was once expressed by the author of a text or that is resident in the pattern of the text. Rather, it is reading that challenges the reader, throws open the reader's world to creative discovery, to new associations that may be suggested as

> much by irrational or chance associations as by the logical relations so carefully studied, for instance, by the structuralists. (Beardslee 1993:222)

This approach to texts suggests that much of the process of meaning making is, in fact, unconscious and, when coupled with a Freudian "hermeneutic of suspicion," gives rise to a postmodernist psychoanalytic critique of the sort developed by Stephen Moore. Other psychoanalytic critics such as Jacques Lacan, Julia Kristeva, and Luce Irigaray explore the nonrational dimensions of language, the unconscious associations of signifier and signified, and the pre-verbal dimensions of language, sound and rhythm, that contribute to meaning (Aichele et al. 1995:187–224).

Rhetorical criticism analyzes the structures of a text in terms of how an author seeks to produce a desired effect in the reader—to persuade, affirm, or call for decision. While rhetorical critics seldom use overtly psychological categories or language, clearly any theory of rhetoric, ancient or modern, contains implicitly some theory of human cognition. In order to influence another's thoughts, attitudes, or will, one builds on assumptions about how those thoughts, attitudes, or intentions are formed and how the interaction of one individual with another will shape or influence them. Whether exploring the conventions of early Greco-Roman rhetoric or investigating the patterns of persuasion for the modern reader, rhetorical critics are engaged in a form of psychological biblical criticism.

The World in front of the Text

Above all, it is in relation to the world in front of the text that psychology comes into its own. For Ricoeur, the movement of explanation, of analyzing the structure of the text, must reach its conclusion in appropriation, in the interpreter's ability "to understand oneself in front of the text" (1991:88). Appropriation takes place in the imaginative space between the interpreter's own world and the possible world projected by the text. It is controlled neither by the "objectivity" of the text itself—referential or structural—nor by the subjectivity of the reader but is a negotiation among them.

Paul Pruyser has described this interaction with reference to "illusion processing." Pruyser expanded on work by object-relations theorist D. W. Winnicott on "transitional objects," such as a child's teddy bear or blanket.

Transitional objects serve as essential devices in a child's transition from egoistic self-orientation to a healthy ability to relate to the external world. Taking Winnicott's suggestion that religion serves in this intermediate area of transitional phenomena, Pruyser proposed an "illusionistic world" between the autistic world of subjective experience and the realistic world of objective experience. The realistic world is based on sense perceptions, while the autistic world is characterized by unfettered fantasy. The illusionistic world, he suggests, is characterized by "tutored fantasy," which is still open to imaginative possibility, but the imagination is orderly and communicable to others. Where the realistic world is based on "look-and-see" referents and the autistic world in ineffable images, the illusionistic world offers verbalizable images. Between the work of the realistic and the dreamworld of the autistic lies the play world of the illusionistic (Pruyser 1991c).

Offering the opportunity for imaginative interplay and communication in symbolic transactions with others, the illusionistic world is the ground of art, music, literature, and religion (and thus of both psychology and hermeneutics). Pruyser's illusion processing is reminiscent of Gadamer's analogy of hermeneutics as *play*. Play takes place "in between" the players and the rules of the game. The game exists as a potential pattern; the potential of the game is only actualized when players enter into it and allow themselves to "be played" by the game. Art belongs to this kind of play (Gadamer 1992). Distortion of the illusionistic world in the direction of either of the other two damages the capacity for relatedness. In autistic distortion, there is a neurotic compromise between wishful thinking and reality, giving rise to both ethereal images of heaven and the aggressive fantasies of slaughtered enemies characteristic of apocalyptic thinking (Pruyser 1991b). Realistic distortion in the form of concretizing symbolic language gives rise to fundamentalism and the doctrine of the inerrancy of scripture in religion, and "the intellectual narrowness of positivism" in science (Pruyser 1991a:113).

We have already noted the close relationship between psychological biblical criticism and reader-response and ideological criticism. Both of these methods involve the relationship between reader and text in the world in front of the text; they ask how a reader is affected by reading and what cognitive and meaning-making processes go into the act of reading.

Reader-response criticism highlights the interaction of the reader and the text, both on what the reader brings to reading and how the process of reading changes the reader. Explicitly psychological-response perspectives have been brought to bear on literature by Norman Holland and David Bleich (Holland 1968, 1973, 1975; Bleich 1978, 1988). Holland particularly examines the way that a reader's personality or self-consciousness affects his or her interpretation of a text. Readers, Holland argues, employ "defensive structures" to preserve their sense of identity. In the end, he asserts, "we use the literary work to symbolize and finally to replicate ourselves" (1976:342).

Whether texts reinforce or challenge readers, they have effects on the readers' thoughts, attitudes, perspectives, and volition. Each of these factors has psychological dimensions, leading Wayne Rollins to suggest that, in addition to considering the *Sitz-im-Leben*, or original historical setting of a text, we must also pay attention to the *Nachleben* of the text, the impact it has had on individuals and cultures over time. Concern for the impact of the text on present readers, in contrast to historical-critical concern for ancient settings, customs, and conventions allows the psychological critic to connect more directly with contemporary readers. Psychological biblical interpretations have been offered more by psychologists and pastoral counselors than by conventional biblical scholars. Present readers are far more accessible for study and reflection than an ancient writer.

We have already noted the significance of Freud for the development of a hermeneutic of suspicion that undergirds ideological criticism, as well as the similarities between psychological criticism and one form of ideological criticism: feminist reading. Ideological criticisms seek to unmask the ways in which a text constructs worldviews and the impact that those constructions have on communities and individuals. Such analysis touches on questions of cognition, perceptual frameworks, and behavior—all fruitful dimensions for psychological insight.

FINAL METHODOLOGICAL OBSERVATIONS

Ricoeur describes the reciprocal movements of explanation and understanding in hermeneutics: "Hermeneutics seems to me to be animated by this double motivation: willingness to suspect, willingness to listen; vow of rigor, vow of obedience" (1970:27). Psychological hermeneutics can both serve as analysis and critique of unconscious dimensions of the text and can lead toward re-engagement and transformation of the reader.

At its best, psychological biblical criticism can mediate between the relatively objective dimensions of the text and the personality and interpretive strategies of the reader. It requires careful analysis of what the text says and does not say, "to allow the world of being that is the 'thing' of the biblical text to unfold" (Ricoeur 1975:95–96). To do this, it is necessary to make use of all the interpretive tools of linguistic, structural, stylistic, and historical criticism, adding an informed sensitivity to the psychodynamics of human interaction, communication, and symbolization. A multidisciplinary approach serves as a deterrence to psychologism, a reduction of all phenomena to psychological categories. The multiple complexities of the text, its origins, and its effects can no more be exhausted by psychology than they can by history, social forces, politics, theology, or any other discipline.

In addition, psychological biblical criticism must give careful attention to the level of the text it is seeking to interpret and acknowledge its limitations, particularly as a method of getting at the historical and psychic world behind the text. Too many attempts to read the Bible psychologically have foundered on the confusion of narrative with history, or of the reader's response with the reference of the text.

Finally, psychological hermeneutics has much to gain from dialogue among differing psychological theories. The methodological pluralism we have mentioned can give the interpreter a parallax view, which will deepen not only the perspective on the text but clarify the strengths and weaknesses of diverse theories.

The most systematic illustration of these considerations can be found in Gerd Theissen's *Psychological Aspects of Pauline Theology*. Theissen is careful to focus his attention on Paul's theology and not his psyche, that is, the world of and in front of the text rather than behind it. For each of the texts in question, he begins with a textual analysis, including psychologically informed categories alongside structural and linguistic points. Second, he does a tradition analysis, drawing on parallels from other ancient Near Eastern cultures, to provide an appropriate context for reflection. Finally, he analyzes the psychological dynamics of the texts in light of three distinctively different psychological theories: learning theory (modified behaviorism), depth psychology, and cognitive theory. In a brief epilogue, he suggests how these theories might illuminate the potential of Paul's theology to transform the reader. Theissen's closing words constitute a declaration of the necessity for psychologically informed hermeneutics: "Anyone who thinks that this religion can be illuminated historically and factually, without psychological reflection, is just as much in error as one who pretends that everything about this religion can be said in this fashion" (1987:398). No one has yet undertaken a study of an Old Testament text similar to Theissen's. In the following chapters, a comparison of several psychological approaches to Genesis 2–3 will be offered, but it will not attempt the kind of integration of psychological theories that Theissen offers.

A SURVEY OF APPROACHES

Prescientific Biblical Psychology

Before the birth of modern psychology, and especially before the profound impact of Freud and depth psychology, biblical psychology was still very much in evidence. R. S. Peters and C. A. Mace suggest that psychology can be divided into three broad categories: presystematic psychology, systematic but prescientific psychology, and scientific psychology (Rollins 1999:7–9). The first stage consists of folk wisdom and intuitions about human behavior and motivations. As an artifact of centuries of observation and interpretation of human living, the Bible contains a wealth of this kind of psychological reflection. Whenever the text mentions the workings of the heart, the purposes of the mind, the intent of an action, love, hate, or anger, it makes psychological statements.

The next phase, systematic but prescientific psychology, can be traced in the development of psychology as a "science of the soul." Early Christian writers like Tertullian and Augustine wrote extensively on the habits, nature, and shaping of the soul, or psyche. In his work *De anima* ("Concerning the Soul"), Tertullian examined the interactions of sense perception and mind and how they produce knowledge, explored the role of the heart as a unifying and guiding dimension of personality, and pondered the nature of sleep and dreams.

Augustine of Hippo considered the knowledge of the soul to be second in importance only to the knowledge of God. His works included *De anima et eius origine* ("Concerning the Soul and Its Origin"), *De immortalitate anime*, ("Concerning the Immortality of the Soul"), and *De duabus animabus* ("Concerning the Two Souls"). His method is introspective and experiential, and from his self reflection he described five broad levels of the psyche: the vegetative, the sensible, the discursively rational, the ethical, and the intellectual. He distinguished between "irrational" dimensions of the soul (appetite, sense perception, anger, and desire) and "rational" dimensions (mind and will).

The field of psychology continued to develop as a subdiscipline of theology; the term *psychology* itself was coined in the sixteenth century to describe, along with natural theology, angelography, and demonology, the three branches of pneumatology, or the doctrine of spirits. Shortly after, the term *anthropology* was created to refer to the science of persons, having the subdivisions of psychology (science of mind) and somatology (the science of the body). Philipp Melanchton, Luther's disciple, was notable in introducing the term to the academic world through his extensive lectures and writings.

Franz Delitzsch, the noted biblical scholar and professor at the University of Leipzig, published *A System of Biblical Psychology* in 1861, just before Wilhelm Wundt opened the way for scientific psychology when he founded his laboratory for psychological research at Leipzig in 1879. His book provides a comprehensive exposition of the issues of concern to systematic biblical psychology before the scientific period: the nature and origin of the soul; the relationship of sin, shame, and conscience; development of the self; waking, sleeping, and dreaming; and conscious and unconscious processes of grace and regeneration (1966). Delitzsch employs many terms that would come to characterize the new psychology, such as "archetypes," the "ego," and "conscious and unconscious dimensions."

Just after the turn of the century, M. Scott Fletcher sought to apply the newly emerging forms of psychological thought specifically to the New Testament, focusing his work on the psychological terminology of the New Testament, psychological experiences described in the text, and theories of personality (1912). No one undertook a similar comprehensive approach to the Old Testament; nonetheless, several attempts were made to explore dimensions of experience and personality in relation to those texts. Of particular interest to several writers were the "ecstatic" or "pathological" qualities of the prophets (Joyce 1910; Kaplan 1906, 1908; Thomas 1914). After the 1920s, scientific psychology became more developed methodologically and more directly reflective of specific schools of theory.

Psycholinguistics, the Brain, and Behaviorism

Most of the research in brain functioning does not deal directly with the Bible but can provide background for understanding how perception, language, and cognition work. Studies on memory provide some insight into the means of oral transmission of religious traditions, and J. Steyn critiqued discourse analyses of ancient texts from the perspective of psycholinguistic theory (Abel 1971; Bradshaw 1981; Ong 1982; Steyn 1984).

Julian Jaynes drew on biblical examples, among others, to illustrate his theory that consciousness developed from a "bicameral mind," in which there was no direct communication between the two hemispheres of the brain (1976). While not affirming Jaynes's bicameral theory, H. Schneidau built on Jaynes's observation that consciousness is a "narratizing" of experience to ask how the Bible as narrative has shaped the consciousness of modernity (1986).

Research on lateral specialization in the brain also provides the context for F. B. Wood's conclusion that biblical faith is related to left-hemisphere function (1988). While his examples are all drawn from the New Testament, Walter Wink's proposal that incorporating creative and imaginative methods serves to enable a transformational Bible study is based partly in lateral specialization (1980).

Behavioral theories have been applied to biblical texts in a limited way. Studies have been limited to descriptions of behavior-modification principles that seem to be reflected in the Bible. It is somewhat problematic to describe such readings as typically "behavioristic," as those who apply them are often conservative Christians who reject "theoretical" behaviorism, with its deterministic assumptions, and opt instead for a "methodological" behaviorism, which resembles "common sense" more than scientific investigation. R. Bufford argued that the Bible is preeminently a book about human behavior, while Bolin and Goldberg laid out some foundational issues relating behavioral studies and the biblical text (Bufford 1977, 1978, 1981; Bolin and Goldberg 1979). L. Gruber identified a process of behavioral modification in Moses' dealing with his speech impediment (1986). The behavioral concept of "learned helplessness," based on the observation of experimental animals subjected to unpredictable stress who began to evidence an impaired ability to adapt, has been applied to Job (Reynierse 1975a, 1975b) and Saul (Van Praag 1986). These studies suffer from the difficulty of assessing whether the human situation in fact parallels laboratory animal experiments and disregard for the limits inherent in the text itself. Van Praag goes as far as to suggest that Saul's behavior shows evidence of the type of brain damage that is sometimes associated with experimental stress in animals.

Freud and Psychoanalysis

Freudian theory has had an enormous impact on biblical interpretation both consciously and unconsciously. It has been applied in a number of ways: as an avenue of investigation into the meaning of symbols and language, as a method of interpreting myth and legend by analogy to dreams and fantasies, and as the ground for the "hermeneutic of suspicion," which warns against taking texts at their face value and challenges interpreters to dig more deeply behind the texts. We shall take a closer look at these issues in relation to the interpretation of Genesis 2–3 in chapter 4.

Dominique Stein describes the factors that should govern psychoanalytic readings: the whole text needs to be considered "like the manifest content of a dream," but it is not necessary to find a latent meaning for each aspect. Attention must be paid to "the gaps, the discordances, the slips in the text, deemed to be as significant as the avowed message"; and the relationship of symbolic representations to unconscious material must be noted, similar to the interpretation of dreams, symptoms, or fantasies. She cautions against "imposing the grid" of theory on the text ("exegesis has nothing to expect from psychoanalysis") but calls for a reader-response analysis. The interpreter will "have created a new work, subject to the consistence and demands of the text, but new nevertheless" (1980:30).

Freudian analysis has often been applied to biblical personalities (often with confusion of the worlds of and behind the text). Zeligs analyzes Moses, Jacob, and other Old Testament figures, finding in them evidences of oedipal conflicts (1974, 1986). Vonck explores Jacob's battle with the figure at the Jabbok, while Kelman examines the dream process at work with Pharaoh's dreams in Exodus (Vonck 1984; Kelman 1986). Anderson describes the pathology that he discerns among the prophets and David (1927), while Fingert concentrates on the personality of Jonah, ignoring the difficulties of discerning whether Jonah is a historical figure or a literary one (1954). No such confusion is evident in Ilona N. Rashkow's exploration of sexuality and family in the patriarchs. She clearly lays out the relationship between psychological theory and reader-response literary theory to guide her investigations of issues of incest, sibling rivalry, and family relations (2000).

Psychological critics have especially been intrigued by the figure of the prophet Ezekiel. Broome prompted a firestorm of controversy when he suggested that many of the troubling aspects of Ezekiel's career could be understood with reference to his psychopathology. Halperin recently revisited Ezekiel with far more careful attention to the development of the text and the factors of the historical setting. His book is a solid example of the contributions that can be made to interpretation by appropriate psychological methods (1993).

Chance reads the book of Ruth in terms of psychodynamic factors in the in-law relationship (1987). Others have found different aspects of the book of Job compelling. Bakan relates it to themes of sacrifice (1968), Katz explores the sense of "dread" described in Job 3:25 (1958), while Goitein ponders the lessons that book may have for the practice of psychoanalysis (1954).

In addition to personalities, psychoanalytic readings have been brought to bear on myths and stories. We will examine this aspect more fully in the chapter on Freudian analysis in the second part of the book.

Freud's disciples modified his views in varying ways, some becoming leaders of divergent schools of thought. Each of these has provided a potential framework for interpretation. Theodor Reik turned his attention to Jewish ritual and tradition, and wrote extensively on issues of biblical interpretation. He made extensive analyses of Genesis 3 (which we will consider later), Moses, the role of Eve, the nature of temptation, and the role of dogma (1951, 1957, 1959, 1960, 1961, 1973). Wohlgelernter drew upon Alfred Adler's concept of "goal-directedness" to describe how Job overcomes his tragic situation (1988). Karen Horney's descriptions of mechanisms for coping with "basic anxiety" have been applied both to biblical figures and to interpreters themselves. Cole describes Cain in terms of Karen Horney's category of "neurotic functioning"(1978), while Zabriskie uses those same categories to understand how different interpreters read biblical passages in relation to women (1976).

Erich Fromm began as an orthodox Freudian but went on to incorporate insights from Marx and other social theorists to illuminate the social dimensions of religion. In his book *You Shall Be as Gods* (1966), he describes the Hebrew Bible as a "revolutionary book" and traces what he perceives as an evolution of consciousness from a tribal society claiming a god above idols to a religion based on a nameless God, enabling human unity and freedom.

French Psychoanalysis: Berguer, Lacan, and Girard

Psychoanalysis as it developed in France has always had a slightly different flavor. Freud himself studied psychology under Jean Martin Charcot at the Salpêtrière neurological clinic in Paris. In more recent years, Jacques Lacan has become influential in France, transforming Freudian theory away from a base in biological drives to symbolic desire for recognition from others. The major task of human development concerns gaining the ability to relate to others as genuinely other, mediated by language and social and cultural symbols. Lacan's theory provides the framework for Piskorowski's interpretation of Genesis 2–3 as a search for the father, Parker's investigation of the same text, and Rashkow's book mentioned earlier (Piskorowski 1992; Parker 1999; Rashkow 2000).

A second influential thinker in French social psychology is René Girard. Girard's anthropological psychology highlights mimetic desire—the universal tendency to imitate others' actions and attitudes unconsciously in order to seek gratification. This leads to mimetic rivalry as desires compete both within the individual and with others and, in turn, unfolds in increasing violence in the social world. The social mechanism for defusing the explosive potential of mimetic rivalry is scapegoating and sacrifice, which unite the rivals against a perceived common enemy. Girard applies his principles explicitly to the reason for Job's suffering (1987).

C. G. Jung and Analytical Psychology

Perhaps the most famous of the Freudian "defectors," Carl Jung differed from the beginning with Freud on a number of points, including the nature of religion. His analytical psychology opens a welcoming space for religious reflection and biblical study. Rollins has described in detail the role of the Bible in Jung's personal formation and its potential contributions to biblical study (1983). Jung's own writings are replete with biblical quotes and allusions; in fact, ten pages of the index to Jung's *Collected Works* are devoted to biblical citations alone, not including additional allusions to biblical persons, stories, symbols, and theology.

Jung recognized clearly the need for a psychological understanding of the Bible; his was one of the voices raised in concern at the state of biblical criticism:

> one can interpret certain biblical texts in many ways. Nor has scientific criticism of the New Testament been very helpful in enhancing belief in the divine character of the holy scriptures . . . under the influence of a so-called scientific enlightenment great masses of educated people have either left the Church or become profoundly indifferent to it. If they were all dull rationalists or neurotic intellectuals the loss would not be regrettable. But many of them are religious people, only incapable of agreeing with the existing forms of belief. (Jung 1969:¶34)

Jung himself wrote his only focused and extended effort at biblical interpretation with *Answer to Job* (to which we shall return below), but the extension of his perspectives has informed a multitude of subsequent works. By far the bulk of the literature has been devoted to archetypal analysis of biblical figures and symbols. Broad studies of Old Testament themes have included Diel's study of biblical symbols, Kluger's reflections on themes of the chosen people, King Saul and the Queen of Bathsheba, and Westman's explorations of the development of consciousness and creativity (Diel 1986a, 1986b; Kluger 1974; Westman 1961, 1983). Biblical personalities again find interpretation through Jungian spectacles: Satan (Dreyfus 1972; Kluger 1967), Jacob and Esau (Cohen 1983), Jacob alone (Kille 1995; Sanford 1981; Wink 1978), Joseph and his dreams (Walsh 1983; Watt 1995), King Saul (Sanford 1985), and Job (Vogels 1981, 1983). Relationships between the masculine and feminine in the God image and the religious history of Israel form the center of studies of the books of Esther (Sigal 1990) and Ruth (Kluger and Kluger-Nash 1999).

The particular dynamics of individuation as described by Jung are the guiding concern of Jungian analyst Edward Edinger, who traces individuation themes from creation through the patriarchs, kings, and prophets to exile and restoration (1972, 1986). J. W. Roffey has found them in relation to the story of the fall, G. Dreyfus and J. Reimer in connection to Abraham, and V. L. Shepperson in the story of Jacob (Roffey 1987; Dreyfus 1995; Shepperson 1984). Jung's methods of amplification and active imagination are evident in Rabbi Levi Meier's retelling of the Jacob story (1994) and in Nomi Kluger-Nash's companion essay "Standing in the Sandals of Naomi," which provides a counterpoint to her father's more analytical study of Ruth (Kluger-Nash 1999).We will take a closer look at Jungian psychology and its role in biblical interpretation in chapter 5.

Other Approaches

Depth psychology has provided a fertile breeding ground for biblical interpretation far beyond any other systems of psychology. Once we move beyond depth psychology, we find ourselves in Wulff's "hopelessly diffuse" arena in which the "single, incidental" incursion is the rule.

Leon Festinger's investigation of cognitive dissonance in contemporary apocalyptic movements highlighted the defense mechanisms that people use to reduce the conflict between expectation and reality. Carroll has applied Festinger's research to Old Testament prophecy (1977, 1980).

Social psychology and family systems theory has been used to examine the dynamics of biblical families (Charny 1973; Rogers 1979). An approach through transactional analysis describes "script formation" in the Bible (Fagan 1976; Lawrence 1983). Literatherapy suggests the Exodus story as a metaphor for therapy (Shiryon 1992). In chapter 6 we will see how Erik Erikson's developmental theories have been applied to Genesis 2–3. There are many other fragmentary and incidental applications that reflect no discernable system.

SOME FINAL CONSIDERATIONS

The Psychological Meaning of "Scripture"

We have seen a variety of dimensions of psychological hermeneutics that will provide fruitful ground for future research. In addition to particular applications of psychological perspectives to individual texts, work is needed to explore the relationship of the personality of the interpreter to his or her choice of method and style of application. Further explication of the hermeneutical, social, and historical dimensions of psychology itself will deepen our understanding of its application to Scripture.

A significant issue in this context that has yet to be adequately explored is the psychological function of the Bible as Scripture. Islamic scholar W. C.

Smith suggested that the ubiquity of sacred Scriptures in religious life suggests "some almost common human propensity to scripturalize" and asked what it may mean historically, sociologically, and psychologically to separate a body of literature from all others and consider it "sacred." Traditional historical-critical study of the Bible deals with the prescriptural phase of the Bible; current criticism tends to read postscripturally. What insights might psychology offer to illumine the peculiar impact of texts on readers who experience them as sacred?

A Methodology for Psychological Biblical Criticism?

Our foray into the theoretical orientations, textual issues, and potential applications of psychological interpretation simply underscores the fact that it is not possible to speak of *a* methodology for psychological biblical criticism. Rather, we face an array of tools, approaches, and perspectives that can offer inroads into the biblical texts. Each psychological theory will bring its own assumptions, framework, and perspective to the task of interpretation. It is when these tools are chosen and applied appropriately, in conjunction with other tools at our disposal, including historical, sociological, and literary tools, that psychological criticism yields the most fruit.

3
Exploring Genesis 3

The story of the Garden of Eden (Gen 2:4b—3:24) has had a wider and more varied impact on Western culture than perhaps any other single Bible text. The images of Adam and Eve, the "forbidden fruit," the tempting serpent, and the trees of life and knowledge have so permeated art, literature, and even popular consciousness that even those who have no biblical or theological interest recognize and understand them. Paul Morris calls the Eden story "*the* text of Western men and women," one that has a "unique significance in the history of our ever-expanding culture . . ." (1992:21).

What might we discover if we were to compare several psychological approaches to a single text? Such a comparison offers an opportunity to highlight the potential strengths and weaknesses of psychological biblical criticism. A comparison of studies of the same text from differing theoretical orientations will serve to highlight methodological issues and hermeneutical strategies of psychological criticism. To date, there have been few efforts to bring together diverse psychological interpretations of the Bible. A few works have compared readings from one limited corner of psychology (usually depth psychology) (Cunningham 1991; Miller 1983), vehemently refuted psychological readings (Heschel 1962; Klein 1956), or borrowed indiscriminately from various theories to serve an author's own purpose. Even fewer have attempted to draw together exegeses of the same biblical text employing differing psychological theories to illuminate not only the psychological dynamics in the text but also the hermeneutical strategies of psychological criticism as a whole.

In the examples in this book, we will limit psychological biblical criticism to a critical reading and interpretation of a biblical text from the standpoint of, and with explicit reference to, a specific psychological theory. It includes both exegesis and hermeneutics. Exegesis is broadly defined as analysis of the biblical text for the purpose of meaningful interpretation. It includes as many aspects of the text as possible, including linguistic, historical, literary, and social as well as psychological aspects. The terms "exegesis" and "hermeneutics" will be used somewhat interchangeably; however, the former will generally refer to critical analysis and the latter to efforts at understanding it.

Genesis 3 presents a particularly fruitful text for psychological interpretation for many reasons. As one of the foundational myths of Western culture, it serves to describe and define the relationships between God and humanity, men and women, and human beings and the world. Its symbols and personalities have become deeply embedded in art and literature, appearing not only in the Sistine Chapel but in daily comic strips. Something in this story seems to speak to the human psyche across cultures and millennia. It is fascinating how the images and motifs of the tale have "escaped" from the garden into popular culture. The apple (or forbidden fruit), the snake, and the figures of Adam and Eve appear in advertising, corporate logos, sexually oriented businesses, real estate, and literature. For example, Apple Computer's apple logo is conspicuously bitten (Morris 1992).

By means of these intriguing symbols Genesis 3 tells a story of sexuality and guilt, of rebellion and estrangement, all issues of great interest to many psychologists. For these reasons, Genesis 3 has prompted a sizeable body of psychological criticism by psychologists and biblical scholars alike.

Within biblical studies generally, the literature on Gen 2:4b—3:24 is overwhelming. Fifty years ago, John McKenzie marveled at the immensity of commentary on the paradise narrative. A survey of the literature in 1913 ran to over 600 pages. McKenzie had in mind only critical literature; if we add to this the store of precritical commentary and expressions and interpretations in art and literature, the size and extent of the material is unimaginable. One could not hope to give full attention to all the twists and turns of interpretation or centuries of expressions in art, literature, and culture. Nor would much of this history of interpretation have any direct bearing on our present concern with psychological interpretation. However, a brief overview of key issues in the interpretation of the Genesis text will serve to highlight significant issues and questions that the text has provoked. These are issues that psychological criticism seeks to answer in its own way.

INTERPRETATION OF GENESIS 3

The Text

Gen 2:4b—3:24 comprises a distinct and self-contained unit of narrative in the primeval history of Genesis 1–11. The whole passage unfolds in reference to a unique place—"a garden in Eden" (2:8). It begins with God placing the newly created human being in the garden and ends with the irrevocable expulsion of the man and woman from Eden (3:24). Despite its reasonably clear beginning and end, the story does not proceed smoothly. In an abrupt shift of focus at the beginning of chapter 3, the previously unmentioned serpent enters as a new character and initiates a new set of events centered not on creation but on the disobedience of the man and woman and its consequences.

We can see two main subthemes within the story: the theme of creation and the theme of disobedience and its consequences. Although the two themes can be roughly distinguished from each other, the author has woven them together so skillfully that it is not possible to separate them completely. The creation story provides the background of relationships and setting against which the disobedience narrative is worked out; disobedience moves the creation story into the next stage.

Woven throughout the story is another puzzling element. Two trees are mentioned: the "tree of the knowledge of good and evil" and the "tree of life." Yet at times it seems as if they are one and the same tree. What is the relationship between the two and how are they connected with life and death?

Early Interpretation

Biblical and Intertestamental Writings. It seems odd that a story that has occupied such a central place in Western tradition attracted very little attention in early Jewish and Christian literature. There is no further mention of the tale in the Hebrew canon. Eve disappears completely after Genesis 4, and Adam appears only in genealogical listings. "Eden" reappears in Hebrew Scriptures as the image of ultimate plenty and fertility, the restored land of Israel. The tree of life resurfaces as an image in Proverbs, used metaphorically to describe desirable qualities. Its companion, the tree of the knowledge of good and evil, disappears completely.

It is in the deuterocanonical and intertestamental books that the familiar associations and expansions of the story begin to develop (Levison 1988). Adam and Eve are invoked in support of marriage (Tob 8:6); the serpent is identified with the devil (Wis Sol 2:23-24); and Eve is identified as the one responsible for sin's entry into the world (Sir 25:24). Other intertestamental writings elaborate the details of the story (Jub 3) and continue the transformation of the Garden of Eden into an image of the heavenly or future paradise. These themes, the marriage relationship of Adam and Eve (with its implicit sexuality), the serpent as devil or Satan, Eve's particular culpability, and Eden as paradise appear frequently in later interpretations of the text.

Early Christian Writings. During the first few centuries of the common era, these key themes develop further in noncanonical writings—the apostolic fathers, the pseudepigrapha, and gnostic treatises. Pseudepigraphal works in particular expand on the Genesis narrative. The Latin *Apocalypse of Moses* and the Greek *Life of Adam and Eve* (c. 100 C.E.) imaginatively expand the details of the canonical tale. Again, we find the serpent identified with Satan. Eve's role is emphasized, while Adam's is downplayed or denied entirely. Paradise is elaborated; it is located in the "third heaven" and is the burial place of Adam, Eve, and Abel. Adam's transgression has brought sin and death into the world.

Decisive new issues came into play with the battles of the formative years of Christianity. Debates over Genesis 3 among early Christian leaders centered on two key issues: the nature of Adam and Eve's sin, and just how it affected the world. Some argued that the sin was essentially *sexual*; that it was an act of intercourse that led to their expulsion. Others argued that *disobedience* was at the heart of the sin. As for the effects of the sin, the central question was whether the Eden story should serve as a warning against using one's moral freedom improperly or whether it described a fundamental alteration in human nature, making human beings incapable of righteous action. Though the former position was argued eloquently by such theologians as Gregory of Nyssa (330–395), Pelagius (c. fourth–fifth century), and John Chrysostom (347–407), the latter view became the prevailing position of the Christian church largely through the efforts of Augustine of Hippo (354–430).

Augustine argued vehemently that Adam's actions in the garden carried with it consequences of sexual desire, physical death, and "original sin." No longer were human beings free not to sin; the events of Eden had effected a fundamental change in the structure of the universe. In the fifth century, the church accepted Augustine's interpretation, and the ideas of "sin and fall" have dominated orthodox Christian interpretation of Genesis 3 ever since.

Gnostic Interpretation

The orthodox position was worked out partly in opposition to the Gnostics. The gnostic view not only contradicted the "sin and fall" position, but completely reversed the usual understanding of the text. Far from recounting the fall of humanity, gnostic writers proclaimed, the Eden story instead concerns humanity's rebellion against the deceptive rulers (Archons) of this world and a return to the original union of soul and spirit (Pagels 1988). Adam and Eve represent aspects of human soul and spirit; death has come about because of their separation and will only be overcome by their reunion. To achieve this, Adam must defy the evil Archons who wish him to remain ignorant; aided by the wise serpent, he must eat from the tree of knowledge.

Modern Critical Approaches

Few other texts in the Bible have received more attention in modern biblical studies than Genesis 3. With each new critical method, scholars have answered previous questions in their own terms and raised new ones. Although expressed in different language, and interpreted in new ways, the same themes about the text continue to be elaborated.

Historical-Critical Interpretation. Historical-critical approaches have sought to understand the text in terms of its historical context and development. Critics saw disjunctions or anomalies in the text as evidence for differing historical sources. Was Genesis 2–3 originally one unified tradition or a combination of two separate sources: one dealing with creation and the other with disobedience? Was the description of the rivers that flow from Eden (2:10-14) an interruption that seems to have no immediate narrative purpose, part of the original source, or taken from elsewhere? Do the sometimes inconsistent and awkward references to the two trees indicate the joining of different traditions? What were the origins, development, and transmission of the traditions before they entered written form? Historical critics looked also to parallel themes and language in other parts of the Old Testament, notably the Wisdom literature, and in ancient Near Eastern texts, particularly the Enuma Elish, the Gilgamesh epic, and the tale of Adapa.

In historical-critical studies, the issues of sexuality and the nature of the transgression emerge cloaked in historical terms. Some interpreters emphasized the role of the sacred tree and the serpent as sexual images and read the story as a warning against Israelite involvement in Canaanite fertility cults. Others, noting close similarities between the theme and vocabulary of this text and those of Wisdom literature, saw it either as part of Wisdom traditions or as a polemic against them. Still others discerned a political issue at stake—the prerogative of the ruling elite represented by God's ownership of the garden—and the evil of rebellion against the established order.

Literary Interpretation. Literary approaches to the text are interested not so much in the historical context of the story but in its present form: the presence or absence of the narrator, plot movement, character interactions, transformations and internal dynamics of the literary text. Critics have proposed a number of possible outlines for Genesis 2–3 and identified key themes of separation and reunion and the close relationship of the story to transitions in the human life cycle. Separation and differentiation carry forward the themes of Gen 1:1—2:4a (emphasized in wordplays) and shape the development of the figure of Eve. Within the wider context of Genesis 1–11 (the primeval history), the Eden narrative sets in motion a twofold dynamic—the increasing separation of humanity from God and the resulting need for greater human autonomy (Gros Louis 1982).

Structuralist Interpretation. According to structuralist critics, separation and differentiation are embedded in the depths of the text itself. Structuralism assumes that meaning is a function of the network of relationships between the elements of the text. Each element is meaningful only because it differs from other similar elements and as it combines with other elements in interconnected structures. In this tale are found oppositions between heaven and earth, life and death, man and garden, man and animal, tree of life and tree of death (tree of good and evil). The story unfolds within the tension of these opposites (Leach 1969). Edmund Leach suggested that the structure of Genesis 1–4 is similar to that of the Oedipus myth, an association that will prove significant for Freudian interpretations of the text. Structural analysis also points to an inherent tension within the story, supporting contradictory interpretations. Alongside the dominant "sin and punishment" theme, there is also a countermovement in which Adam and Eve in fact gain something of value (Culley 1980).

Reader-Response Interpretation. Linguistic constructions within the text lead the reader to understand it in certain ways, but require a reader to relate those elements to language and cultural codes, to each other, and to the reader's own experience (Wolde 1989). Genesis 3 is tantalizingly lacking in details. The characters are only barely sketched, the actions are simple yet hint at profound significance. Readers cannot help but ask questions. Why is the tree prohibited? Is the knowledge of good and evil received from the tree, or from the very act of disobedience? What were Adam and Eve like before eating the fruit—childlike, unsophisticated, primitive? The text presents a reader with a number of imaginative possibilities. How one "fills in the gaps" in the text will affect his or her exegesis (Gros Louis 1974).

Some of these imaginative possibilities are open and unconditioned by any textual elements, while others are directed and limited by the unfolding narrative. Wordplays are one means of leading the reader, and in the Eden tale there are links of sound and root between words for "nakedness" (*'arumim*), "shrewd" (*'arum*), and "cursed" (*'arur*). Other structures require the reader to choose between conflicting senses. For example, the only point at which the narrator speaks directly is in 2:24: "Therefore a man leaves his father and his mother and clings to his wife, and they become one flesh." One might justly conclude that the process of maturing provides primary focus for the whole narrative section. But how, then, is one to reconcile this positive theme with the seemingly negative events of disobedience and punishment? Is the story fundamentally about a "fall," or a tale of gaining wisdom and autonomy? Ultimately, readers must resolve the tension in their own way. Yet even this freedom may be constrained. As Ellen van Wolde points out, readers are not always "free" to make their own choice. Church tradition since Augustine has consistently insisted on the "sin and fall" axis as compulsory (1989:222).

Feminist interpretation. Ever since Eve was singled out for special condemnation for her role in the events of Eden, Genesis 3 has played a prominent role in forming and justifying patriarchal attitudes toward women in Western society. Feminist approaches to the text seek to counter those attitudes by asking what this text really says about the relationships between men and women. Is it an essentially pro-woman text that has simply been distorted by patriarchal interpretation? Phyllis Trible lists eleven statements representing what she describes as the consensus, but unnecessary, "misogynous reading" of the text (1978). Or are the attitudes of patriarchy so inextricably woven into the language and structure of the tale that they cannot be overcome?

Psychological Criticism

The quantity, breadth, and diversity of interpretation of Genesis 3 testifies to the complexity of this seemingly simple tale. Each approach illuminates some aspect of its possible significance: historical context, literary parallels, wordplay and characterization, semantic structures, and the effect on the reader, shaping attitudes and social relations. Yet, the same questions that concerned early readers continue to shape interpretation today. What, exactly, happened in that garden? What does it have to do with evil, sin, and death? Is it a story about a fall from paradise, or about growing into new human potential? What is the knowledge of good and evil, and why is it prohibited? Does this all have something to do with sexuality? Who is the serpent, and why does it entice the woman? Is it all the woman's fault?

As modern critics have addressed those questions, they have begun to draw upon psychological terms and concepts that are so embedded in modern consciousness. For example, though neither Fishbane nor Trible consider their efforts to be "psychological criticism," both suggest that the story has psychological aspects. Fishbane describes chapter 3 as a "psychological drama" and uses terms like "orality," "projection," and "repression" to describe its dynamics (1979:20–23). Trible outlines the text as a three-part drama of the struggle of life (Eros) and death (Thanatos), acknowledging that she draws these ideas in part from the work of Freud (1978:139, n. 2).

Psychological criticism claims that many of the persistent questions about Genesis 3 have profound psychological implications. Its symbolism and themes express conscious and unconscious dimensions of human experience and behavior that other critical methods have not identified or exhausted. Psychological criticism engages the issues of sexuality, guilt, consciousness (the knowledge of good and evil), separation, and union, and the sense of sin in its own way. In addition, psychological perspectives ask new questions of the text.

Does psychological criticism offer anything unique to the interpretation of Genesis 3? What relationships do psychological interpretations have to other readings? How useful or adequate are psychological approaches?

CRITERIA FOR ADEQUATE INTERPRETATION

Our brief survey of the history of the exegesis of Genesis 3 demonstrates the multitude of interpretations that can be made of a single text. Critical theory has increasingly highlighted the polyvalent, systemic, and interactive qualities of language and the significant impact on interpretation made by readers and ideologies. No longer can any single reading of a text lay easy claim to being *the* meaning. Within this stunning diversity, which often includes mutually contradictory exegeses, can there be any standard to evaluate one reading against another? Is one limited, as some would suggest, to presenting the spectrum of readings as evidence for the diversity of readers or reading communities?

In order to provide a consistent standard of evaluation and a context for comparison, we will turn to the hermeneutical theory of Ricoeur for a set of criteria for adequate interpretation. These criteria will enable us to evaluate our chosen exegeses individually and compare them to each other by understanding their characteristic approaches and discovering their relative strengths and weaknesses. Ricoeur seems appropriate both for the breadth and inclusiveness of his theory, which mediates between text-oriented and reader-oriented approaches, and for his familiarity with the issues of psychology and hermeneutics.

Ricoeur's recognition that language has multiple levels and requires interpretation led him to examine psychoanalysis as a hermeneutical system in *Freud and Philosophy* (1970). Ricoeur considered Freud's theories foundational for a "hermeneutic of suspicion." Freud's findings regarding distortions and illusions in dreams and the unconscious prevent any easy supposition that interpretation is simply a process of recovering the "meaning" packaged in a text. Symbols not only reveal, they can just as easily conceal. Furthermore, symbols can carry more than one message; they are plurivocal, even as dream images are "overdetermined"—revealing or concealing multiple possibilities. Thus, *all* symbols require interpretation, and the human propensity to illusion and "false consciousness" demands from the outset an effort at deciphering and demystification. Psychoanalysis deals with phenomena—individual dreams and neurotic symptoms, and cultural manifestations such as myths, folktales, jokes, and art—which are not immediately recognizable as "texts." Yet they all can be treated as such in that they all participate in interlinked systems of signification and communication and in that they are mediated through language. One can rightly question whether corporate myths are substantively different from individual dreams or fantasies, and whether one can apply the same interpretive methods to both. Individual phenomena are mediated linguistically incidentally because they have to be described to another (the analyst). Myths, however, are more firmly embedded in textuality as they are developed and transmitted through time. As we shall see, several psychological interpretations of Genesis 3 proceed on the basis of the assumption that individual dreams and corporate myths allow for the same interpretative methods.

Suspicion is not the final word, however. The phenomena of the psyche may be veiled, but they are not ultimately unintelligible. The purpose of analysis, critical or psychological, is to work through initial illusion to a new, deeper level of understanding. Interpretation moves from the critique of illusory "false" consciousness toward a realization of "true" consciousness—a widening of awareness that allows the individual to live more fully—through a deciphering of psychic symbols. Ricoeur summarizes this dual purpose thus: "Hermeneutics seems to me to be animated by this double motivation: willingness to suspect, willingness to listen; vow of rigor, vow of obedience. In our time we have not finished doing away with *idols* and we have barely begun to listen to *symbols*" (1970:27).

Ricoeur affirms that texts are inherently polysemic and that there will always be multiple possibilities for interpretation. Not all interpretations are equal, however. He asserts that any given text presents "a limited field of possible constructions." Within this field, "[i]t is always possible to argue for or against an interpretation, to confront interpretations, to arbitrate between them, and to seek agreement, even if this agreement remains beyond our immediate reach" (1976:79). Within this "conflict of interpretations," as

Ricoeur has named it, one can nonetheless suggest criteria to characterize interpretations as more or less successful.

Explanation and Understanding

Ricoeur's hermeneutics occupy a middle ground between theories that identify the primary locus of textual meaning in the intention of the author and those that focus on the role of the reader in constructing meaning. Ricoeur is not willing to allow either extreme of this polarity to dominate interpretation. The act of writing, he contends, removes a text from the realm of conversation in which speaker and hearer share a common context. This "distanciation," inherent in the act of writing, "renders the text autonomous with respect to the intention of the author" (1991:83). The text is, however, not open to *any* interpretation whatsoever. Although language is intrinsically ambiguous and polyvalent, the structures of semantics and text that build words into sentences and sentences into a "work" serve interactively to limit the possible fields of reference of that text. What results from this interaction is a "world in front of the text"—a proposed world that a reader can engage.

For Ricoeur, interpretation involves two simultaneous activities that describe an "arc" ranging between explanation and understanding. Explanation involves critical analysis of the text structures to allow the proposed "world" of the text to unfold, while understanding (or appropriation) describes the process by which a reader comes "to understand oneself in front of the text" (1991:88). The text becomes a new event of discourse, a fresh and present address to the reader in the act of reading.

CRITERIA FOR ADEQUATE INTERPRETATION

If symbols are by nature polyvalent, and multiple interpretations are always possible, is there any basis for evaluating the relative adequacy of different interpretations? Ricoeur answers positively: although texts never have only one possible meaning, some interpretations are better than others. Criteria for evaluation can only assess relative adequacy within the conflict of interpretations.

Ricoeur has not offered a comprehensive list of criteria for valid interpretation. However, in *Interpretation Theory: Discourse and the Surplus of Meaning* and *Metaphor and the Main Problem of Hermeneutics*, he suggests a few key factors within this interplay of explanation and understanding, sense and reference (1976, 1978a).

A more valid interpretation will deal with the text as a whole. One must approach the text as a "work," not just a collection of words. While fairly regular rules and conventions govern the formation of words from phonemes and sentences from words, at the level of the sentence we enter a new level of discourse. Metaphor and symbol begin to work their "double meaning" to create new imaginative possibilities. There is a cumulative effect of expansion and limitation of possible meanings as a text unfolds. For example, a mystery novel depends on a developing sequence of descriptions and actions that lead the reader to re-evaluate what he or she has read in the light of new clues. What once seemed significant becomes trivial; a minor point emerges as a key to the mystery.

At its simplest level, this interrelationship is what we call "context." If I see the word "jack," I can imagine any number of possible meanings—a tool, a child's toy, a playing card, a sailor. When I learn that the jack is in the trunk of a car, that fact leads me to anticipate that it is a tool (though it still could be one of the other objects). Further information that someone took the jack out of the car to change a tire confirms my previous guess and makes the reference clear. At a more subtle level, the style of writing, the historical context of the work, the genre, and other conventions will serve to limit the semantic range of the text. We are all familiar with the problem of "proof texting"—taking a statement out of its context to declare a significance that is beyond or even contrary to the contextual meaning. Indeed, proof texting illustrates how a sentence placed into a new work generates different meanings derived from new interrelationships.

Thus, a valid interpretation is not fragmentary but will address the entire work, noting literary genres, themes, allusions, and other structures. The process of analysis will thus involve both identification of individual components and tracing their interrelationships. This process is always circular; each proposed reconstruction is subject to confirmation or revision in light of subsequent details.

A more valid interpretation will deal with the text as an individual. Although a text may share much in common with other texts of similar literary conventions and common genres, each text is also an individual. What readers appreciate in different texts is not merely the communication of information but the uniqueness (or predictability) of style, language, plot, and characterization. Shakespeare's *Romeo and Juliet* and Bernstein's *West Side Story*, while sharing the same plot and parallel characters, are significantly different works. Placing a text in its appropriate genre is essential; reading the book of Daniel as a prophetic book rather than an apocalyptic book will lead to misreading. Simultaneously, each work will develop its own "world" in relation to, or sometimes in tension with, its genre.

The explanation of a text necessarily involves examining its linguistic and literary structures and comparing them with similar texts. Careful analysis of the structures of the text, literary and mythical, are useful for illuminating such similarities, but one hazard of structural analysis is overgeneralization and reductionism. At some level of abstraction, all texts appear the same. While Genesis 3 may have close similarities to other mythic tales of the origins of evil, it is not identical. An adequate interpretation must identify and explain those elements that distinguish *this* text from all others.

A more valid interpretation will account for the greatest number of factors found in the text and will demonstrate greater convergence between the aspects considered. Ricoeur characterizes a poor explanation as "narrow or far-fetched." A narrow approach will gloss over oddities or perplexities in the text, or will inflate minor details to obscure the overall movement of the text. A far-fetched explanation fails the test of probability in the conflict of interpretations. It must be coherent with our experience or what we know from other sources. For example, while attributing Ezekiel's vision of God's throne (Ezek 1:4-28) to the prophet's encounter with a flying saucer may be quite inventive, such a reference is highly implausible.

In a sense, this criterion is a combination of the two preceding standards. In describing both the typical and unique aspects of the text, a more adequate interpretation will show how those elements relate and interact to produce the work as a whole. It is also a recognition that a (written) interpretation of a text is itself a work of discourse. Here we have begun to move from the discourse, and more narrowly the *sense*, of the text into the broader arena of the potential *reference* of the text. The boundaries between these dimensions are somewhat elastic; we have already invoked such transtextual categories as genre and style. Even more so, as one weighs a given interpretation against others for its relative adequacy, other factors—history, culture, tradition, worldviews—come into play.

Following Ricoeur, biblical scholar Sandra Schneiders has restated some characteristics of this criterion. We can evaluate an interpretation as to whether it can account for the current form of the text, whether it is consistent with itself, and whether it deals with the whole text. Furthermore, in relation to other interpretations, an adequate interpretation will be equal to or more successful at explaining irregularities in the text and will be compatible with what we know about the text from other sources. Schneiders moves well beyond Ricoeur's criteria to suggest additional criteria: a consideration of what cannot be done or left undone, and whether an interpretation responsibly uses all methods that are appropriate within the interpretative framework chosen. These formulations beg the question as to what constitutes "appropriate," "responsible," or "permissible" interpretations and reflect Schneiders's own hermeneutical method (1991:164–67).

No single interpretation can exhaust all the interpretive possibilities of a text. We cannot take any explanation to task for how it does not deal with factors outside its purview. Rather, we ask how adequately it accounts for what it *does* claim to examine, and whether its analysis is relatively narrow or comprehensive.

A more valid interpretation will enable the text to mean all it can mean. Given the fact that the text inherently has many possible meanings and complex multiple interactions within the text, an adequate interpretation will avoid reducing the text to a single aspect or referent. While one may argue that a given factor may be more important than others, other features still affect the development of the discourse of the text. The figures of tree and serpent in Genesis 3, for example, can potentially refer to objects in the natural world, religious symbols of ancient Near Eastern religion, phallic symbols, and more. Any one of these may seem most important, but the others always are hovering in the background. An interpretation that "enables" meaning will honor the richness of potential meaning in the text. It will not simply declare "*x* is *nothing more* than a reference to *y*."

"Enabling meaning" relates to the integration of explanation and understanding. As we have noted above, explanation and understanding are not separate steps in interpretation, but interpenetrate each other every step of the way. Explanation will always flow out of prior understanding; conversely, understanding is shaped and sharpened by explanation. By speaking of "enabling meaning," we have moved well beyond the explanation of the *sense* into the realms of *reference.*

The hermeneutic of suspicion may play a role in expanding the range of potential meanings. By questioning the assumed consciousness of the text (and the reader), such suspicion can reveal hidden factors that shape its interpretation and add to its reservoir of meaning. "Understanding is hermeneutics; henceforward, to seek meanings is no longer to spell out the consciousness of meaning, but to *decipher its expressions.* . . . If consciousness is not what it thinks it is, a new relation must be instituted between the patent and the latent; this new relation would correspond to the one that consciousness had instituted between appearances and the reality of things" (1970:33).

A more valid interpretation will enable appropriation. Such an interpretation will unfold the world in front of the text so that it is intelligible, so that a reader can come to a new self-understanding in the encounter with the text. Hans-Georg Gadamer has characterized the hermeneutical task of understanding as the "fusion of horizons," that is, the intersection of the world of the interpreter with the world of the text (1992). Appropriation involves not only an analysis of various aspects of the text, it requires a re-expression of those elements in a way that the reader can grasp.

Ricoeur's critique of structuralism centers on structuralism's inability (or unwillingness) to move from an explication of the underlying "code" of a text to appropriation of the text's message, that is, explanation without understanding (1975:65). He correctly argues that an interpretation that does not move beyond analysis of linguistic, semantic, and narrative structures into consideration of the truth claims of the text and the potential worldview it projects has left its work incomplete.

INTERPRETING INTERPRETATIONS

Throughout this study, we are clearly dealing with interpretations of interpretations. We must apply Ricoeur's criteria not only to the various texts before us but to the analysis of those exegeses as well. One wagers not only that the explanation of the psychological texts will be appropriate but that the presentation of Ricoeur's own thought (a work comprising many different texts) is itself adequate.

For our purpose of evaluating psychological interpretations Ricoeur thus offers a particularly helpful starting point. His theory occupies a middle ground in hermeneutics between text-oriented and reader-oriented theories, taking seriously both aspects of the hermeneutical process. This middle ground allows one to take seriously both the (relatively) objective phenomenon of the text and the (relatively) subjective dimensions of a reader's personality and experience. Paul Pruyser, working from a foundation in object relations theory and D. W. Winnicott's concept of the "transitional object," describes this interaction between the external "realistic world" and the internal "autistic world" as occupying a third imaginative space, which he terms the "illusionistic world." The illusionistic world corresponds well to Ricoeur's proposed "world in front of the text" as it is appropriated by a reader. Pruyser argues convincingly that all culture, art, and religion occupy this mediating space (Maloney and Spilka 1991). Ricoeur's insistence on the plurivocity of texts and the cumulative sense of a "work" arising out of the interplay of structures allows for many analytical methods—linguistic, generic, narrative, and structural. Also, his insistence on appropriation brings into play transtextual elements of history, consciousness, attitude, and the reader. In seeking to bring convergence out of the "conflict of interpretations," Ricoeur's theories allow room for a more comprehensive spectrum of approaches than any other.

Furthermore, he is familiar with Freud and Freudian theory and has taken seriously the critical implications of Freudian psychological theory for hermeneutics. Freud's observations are foundational not only for psychoanalysis but for other psychological theories and the general worldview of the twentieth-century Western world as well. Finally, though less directly relevant, he himself has ventured an interpretation of Genesis 3 in *The Symbolism of Evil* (1967).

How valid is psychological criticism of Genesis 3? Are some interpretations more fruitful and compelling than others? Do particular psychological theories lend themselves more readily to the interpretation of this text? What might characterize a more or less successful psychological reading of Genesis 3? In the following chapters, we will examine specific readings from perspectives of several psychologies, evaluating their effectiveness in light of Ricoeur's criteria of validity.

The chosen psychological perspectives include Freudian, Jungian, and developmental theories. All three systems lend themselves well to the interpretation of Genesis 3. Freudian and Jungian psychology are both considered "depth psychologies," that is, they include unconscious phenomena and motivations in their considerations. However, they differ significantly in their approach to, and understanding of, those unconscious factors. The term "developmental" is not, strictly speaking, a distinct school of thought in psychology. It refers here to a cluster of theories concerning the development and maturation of personality and would include such theorists as Piaget, Erikson, Fowler, and Winnicott. Although some biblical critics draw implicitly on psychological terms and concepts, we include only those that refer explicitly to psychological theory. To make the methodological characteristics of the three schools clear, we attempt to limit the analyses to those that more faithfully reflect the mainstream of each orientation. Finally, preference is given to longer and more comprehensive treatments, though shorter and more partial essays are cited upon occasion.

4 "A Wretched, Tendentious Distortion": Freud and Psychoanalysis

[I]n all likelihood the myth of Genesis is a wretched, tendentious distortion devised by an apprentice priest, who as we now know stupidly wove two independent sources into a single narrative (as in a dream).

—Freud, quoted in McGuire 1974:473

Sigmund Freud's disdain for the Genesis text, expressed in these words written to Carl Jung in 1911, might explain why he himself never undertook an interpretation of Genesis 3. Despite his assertion that "my deep engrossment in the Bible story had, as I recognized much later, an enduring effect upon the direction of my interest" (1959:8), he himself made few references to the biblical text itself in his work. He paid little explicit attention to the themes of the Bible and dealt at length only with the figure of Moses in *Moses and Monotheism*, a work in which he passed lightly over the biblical text and developed instead his theories of the origins of religion and culture. Freud acknowledges his "autocratic and arbitrary" use of biblical tradition, "bringing it up to confirm my views when it suits me and unhesitatingly rejecting it when it contradicts me. . . ." "But," he adds, "this is the only way in which one can treat material of which one knows definitely that its trustworthiness had been severely impaired by the distorting influence of tendentious purposes. . . . Certainty is in any case unattainable and moreover it may be said that every other writer on the subject has adopted the same procedure" (1964:27, n. 2). Freud's reluctance to engage the Genesis text directly was not shared by his followers, who proposed a number of psychoanalytic interpretations of the story of Adam and Eve. Indeed, it was a paper presented by Sabina Spielrein at the November 29, 1911, meeting of the Psychoanalytic Society in Vienna that prompted Freud's comment to Jung. In that paper, she alluded to Eve's "seduction" of Adam. Freud also mentions an interpretation by Otto Rank, which we will explore below.

Freud's terse comments to Jung represent, unbeknownst to Freud himself, a programmatic outline for subsequent Freudian interpretations. He declares that Genesis is a myth, and as such is like a dream, weaving together differing strands of disparate material. Freudian analysis considers myth to be a collective parallel to an individual's dream, and thus one can apply psychotherapeutic methods of dream interpretation to myths. Dreams (and by analogy, myths) need interpretation because they are symbolic; beneath the evident form and figures of the dream (the "manifest content"), there lies a deeply unconscious meaning that can only be expressed symbolically (the "latent content").

The text, understood as myth or dream, is "a tendentious distortion," owing to a variety of unconscious psychological defense mechanisms that seek to cloak or conceal the latent content of the dream. Such "distortions" may include displacement (substituting one thing for another), inversion (changing something into its opposite), condensation (merging two things into one), or splitting (1953). In his letter, Freud goes on to caution against reading "the surface version" of myths uncritically. It is necessary to "find our way back to their latent, original forms by a comparative method that eliminates the distortions they have undergone in the course of their history." In Ricoeur's terms, interpretation requires a hermeneutic of suspicion that can "decipher" the text.

Freud favors Otto Rank's opinion that the Genesis story has undergone two major reversals. Two features of the story that seem "strange and singular" are the creation of Eve out of Adam (an inversion of the natural order) and the motif of the woman giving a symbol of fertility (the fruit) to the man. If the original myth has been inverted, as Rank suggested, then the giving of the fruit becomes a familiar marriage rite, and Eve is Adam's mother. Thus, Freud notes, "everything would be clear . . . we should be dealing with the well-known motif of mother-incest, the punishment for which, etc." (McGuire 1974:473). While Freud is content to let the matter rest with his "etc.," his followers were all too willing to spell out the details.

FREUDIAN APPROACHES TO MYTH

Freud's letter to Jung anticipates three issues that will characterize subsequent Freudian interpretations of Genesis 3. (1) One must take the story to be myth, and as such, analogous to a dream. (2) As in a dream, the narrative's meaning is presented symbolically. The manifest content conceals unconscious latent contents. Interpretation therefore requires careful analysis of the symbols and their interaction. (3) The latent content of the tale recapitulates an early, repressed stage of human development.

The Oedipal Drama

Most of the authors we will consider agree with Freud's assessment that the latent content of Genesis 3 concerns incest with the mother—the Oedipus complex. The Oedipus complex, a term that has made its way into common usage, is Freud's name for that stage in infant development when a boy (this phase is different for girls) forms an erotic attachment to his mother. He perceives his father as a rival for his mother's affections and wishes to remove him. Either in response to his mother's prohibitions against his touching his penis, or in fear of his father' reprisals, the boy develops "castration anxiety," the fear that the parent will remove his penis (1940:188–93). Freud declares that the Oedipus complex is not only the "nucleus" of individual neuroses, but it is equally the basis for all civilization and religion (1955, 1961a, 1961b, 1964).

The three key components of Freudian approaches are not entirely parallel, nor are they isolated from each other. They refer to different levels of the development and structure of the text. Oedipal dynamics (the latent meaning) are at the root of the story. This root meaning is then transformed and expressed by means of symbols in the form of myth (the manifest content). Thus, Freudian approaches to the text work backward from the mythic text through the symbols to the latent meaning. This is not a neat three-step process; there is an intimate interplay among all three aspects. The assumption that myth is analogous to dreams leads the analyst to seek parallels within other mythic or dream materials. Certain aspects of the individual elements or symbols in the story that emerge from such comparisons then lead to identification of the overall theme as oedipal. The analyst will then draw upon additional elements from oedipal dynamics to expand and clarify further the interpretation of symbols in the narrative.

Myths and Dreams

Freudian interpreters all act on the assumption that all myths, including Genesis 3, are of similar origin regardless of history and culture, and that one must deal with myths as if one were dealing with a dream. Theodor Reik, for example, declares, "There is at least one kind of collective production that can be compared to . . . individual fantasies. They contain, distorted and transformed by changes during thousands of years, memories from an early phase of human evolution: I mean the myths" (1957: 48).

This implicit assumption reveals itself in the way that Freudian commentators summon mythological and dream material equally to support their interpretations. We may discover not only comparisons to material from the ancient Near East but to stories from such wide-ranging sources as the Talmud, Greek and Roman myth and ritual, and myths from India, northern Europe, the South Pacific, and Africa. In the same way, these writers often consider aspects of the text to be parallel to neurotic symptoms, infantile fantasies, and dreams.

Symbolism

Assuming that one can interpret myth just as one interprets dreams means that one must take care to identify and understand the symbols in the story. In Freudian theory, *everything* in a dream is potentially symbolic. Things that one might ordinarily identify as objects in the natural world may represent people, feelings, or events buried deep in the unconscious. Because the meaning of a dream is found in the *latent* content, interpreters pay little attention to the *manifest* content. By means of the Freudian "hermeneutic of suspicion," founded on an accumulated body of case histories, dream symbolism, and world myths, Freudian exegetes propose to "decipher" the text and reveal psychic referents for its various elements.

Commonality of purpose does not necessarily lead to unanimity of interpretation. Although Freudian interpreters have meticulously analyzed the symbolism of the Genesis account, their conclusions are often at variance with one another. Overall, they agree that the symbolism is tied to issues of sexuality. They argue, however, for quite different particular references for symbolic terms.

FREUDIAN INTERPRETATION OF GENESIS 3

Symbolism

Ludwig Levy: Sexual Symbolism. Psychoanalyst Ludwig Levy's effort to decode the passage's sexual symbolism occupies a position on the boundary of conventional historical exegesis and psychological interpretation (1917). In fact, many of Levy's points parallel those of mainstream biblical criticism. Sexual symbolism is not unconscious, he contends, but was carefully chosen by the author and would have been quite clear to the original audience. He illustrates his point with reference to rabbinic, Babylonian, Greek and Roman, and African traditions and tales.

"Eating" is a common euphemism for intercourse, he writes, and the fruit was traditionally considered to be an apple, an erotic symbol corresponding to the female breast. The tree of "knowing" calls to mind how biblical authors use "knowing" as a euphemism for sexual intercourse. "Good and evil" also bears a sexual meaning—in the Hebrew Bible, those who do not know "good and evil" are children and old men, who are not sexually competent. Eating the fruit bestows on the man and the woman the knowledge of their nakedness and feelings of shame (Gen 3:7).

Levy agrees with those who argue that there was only one tree in the garden but sees it as yet another image of sexual knowledge. Sexuality and life are linked—procreation leads to new life, yet also brings death. In dreams, coitus is often a symbol of death. Furthermore, the serpent is a common motif found with the tree of life. It appears as both guardian (in Babylonian images and Greek myth) and tempter (in Genesis). Its role as tempter arises from its function as a phallic symbol. In psychoanalysis, the snake is a familiar erotic image from dreams and neurotic fantasies. At various times and in many cultures around the world the snake represents the phallus. While the serpent may serve as a phallic symbol, Levy cautions against simply substituting the phallus for the serpent in Genesis 3. The serpent here is presented (also) as an actual snake, which can speak with Eve. Their conversation, overshadowed by sexual imagery, operates on two levels: as a "charming" sketch of "feminine psychology" and as a deep description of the experience of sexual awakening.

Levy contends that the curses leveled against the serpent, the woman, and the man become clear in the light of the sexual symbolism throughout the story. God condemns the serpent/phallus to creep on its belly, a refer ence to sexual intercourse. The serpent is doomed to eat earth. As mentioned earlier, "eating" is a euphemism for intercourse; one must take the "earth" here as a reference to the woman—she is the "field" that will be plowed by the man's "plowshare."

Clearly, Levy declares, Eve's punishments relate to her sexual life; her sin must have been sexual. How could painful childbearing correspond to the eating of an apple? Adam's punishment also involves his sexual life, veiled in symbolic language. Ancient communities identified procreation with agriculture. A common vocabulary speaks of sowing (intercourse), seed (semen, offspring), fertilization, and bearing fruit (children). In this correspondence, the woman is the field, the plowshare that plows the field is the phallus, the vulva is the furrow into which the rain/semen falls to produce the fruit/child. Since Adam has sinned by "plowing the field" of Eve, he is now destined to work the literal earth.

Levy concludes by noting that although the author of the Genesis account draws abundantly from the store of sexual symbolism, he has reshaped those symbols according to his overarching theology. The serpent is no divine figure; sexual intercourse is not a holy act, no ritual imitation of the fertility gods of the ancient Near East. Yet while achieving a new level of ethical religion, Jewish tradition (and subsequent Christian teaching) repressed sexuality to a deeply unconscious level. Levy thus unwittingly raises the question of the relationship between myth as an expression of the unconscious, analogous to a dream, and recorded myth as a literary artifact, which has undergone conscious refinement, editing, and literary expression. The task for modern readers, Levy concludes, is to recognize the sexual imagery of the text and to free sexuality from its ancient curse.

Otto Rank: Incestuous Reversal. In his analysis that so influenced Freud, Otto Rank proposes that the story of Eve's creation in Genesis 2 has undergone a reversal to conceal its incestuous origins (1922). Contrary to the manifest form of the tale, Rank asserts that Adam is born from Eve, not vice versa. As "the mother of all living" (Gen 3:20), she is identified with the Primal (Earth) Mother. By analogy to other world parent myths, Eve, the Primal Mother, would be the wife of the sky/creator god Yahweh. Rank notes, however, that some elements of the story also reflect a mythic theme of father-daughter incest and jealousy. Eve plays multiple roles as wife-mother to Adam and wife-daughter to God. The oedipal triangle of mother, father, and son is evident when one realizes that Eve is the Earth, the wife of the sky god Yahweh. Adam is the rebellious son who commits incest with his mother, invoking the wrath of the "injured third"—God.

Rank considers the serpent to be a concealed allusion to the agent of incest. It may refer to Adam, who leads his mother, Eve, into an incestuous sin against God the father. On the other hand, it might represent God, for the serpent functions also as a symbol for father-daughter incest. The serpent is a common phallic symbol appearing in both myths and neurotic fantasies, especially in the context of incest. He does not find it surprising that some Jewish traditions explained that Eve had intercourse with the serpent. In its mythic role as the guardian of the tree (the property of the god/father), the serpent may also symbolize the jealousy of a father guarding his daughter.

The curses on the serpent exemplify the expected punishment for oedipal urgings—castration. Rank cites a rabbinic tradition that the serpent originally stood upright, but its feet are cut off (castrated) as punishment, and it must henceforth crawl on its belly. Rank finds another reference to castration in the unusual creation of Eve. In the manifest form of the story, Eve is created by the removal of Adam's rib. This "rib," he argues, is actually Adam's phallus; the story thus parallels the infantile conception that women are males that have been castrated as punishment.

R. F. Fortune: Genesis and Maori Myth. In an unusual foray into psychohistorical analysis, R. F. Fortune argues that the Genesis narrative can be traced to a distorted version of a Maori myth (1926). Fortune states that Maori oral traditions tell how their ancestors came from Irahia (the Dravidian name for India), and earlier from "Uru," which he takes to be Ur of the Chaldees. The Maori tale, he argues, is an earlier, undistorted form of the Genesis account. In it, an eel sexually excites the first woman with its tail, causing her to seduce Tiki, the first man. In revenge for causing him to fall into the sin of sexuality, Tiki cuts the eel into pieces. This proves, says Fortune, that the serpent is indeed a sexual symbol. Since there are no snakes in New Zealand, the Maori myth substituted the eel. The Genesis account has cloaked and distorted this "original" form of the story, preserved in the Maori tradition, concealing the sexual significance of the serpent and converting the sin into an act of eating the forbidden fruit.

These brief examples show how Freudian interpreters generally did not attend to the text as it stands before embarking on the task of interpreting it. (A notable exception is Theodor Reik, whom we will consider below.) They do not treat it as a *work* but as just one piece in a worldwide puzzle. In Ricoeur's terms, they move prematurely to a search for the reference of the text. In affirming the commonality of the text with a wide spectrum of assumed "parallels," they often gloss over its uniqueness.

Genesis 3 as Oedipal Drama

Just as the assumption that myth and dream are similar leads to a characteristically Freudian approach to symbols, this assumption leads also to a third characteristic of Freudian interpretation. Dreams are cloaked expressions of unconscious material; that material is intimately entwined with early conflicts in human development. The symbols of Genesis 3—husband/wife, mother/son, father/daughter—are all figures from family life, leading our interpreters to the key for understanding in early family dynamics. Mix in symbols of sexuality—serpent and tree—and guilt and punishment, and one has set the stage for a fundamental concern of Freudian theory: the Oedipus complex. Géza Róheim, A. Fodor, and Gudrun Jork interpret Genesis 3 in terms of the Oedipus complex. The fourth study considered below will be that of Theodor Reik. While also describing oedipal dynamics in the text, Reik does so in reference to Freud's myth of the primal horde.

Freudian critics who interpret the Genesis story in terms of the Oedipus complex argue, unlike Levy, that symbolism in the narrative is unconscious, and that it conceals levels of the story not evident to the original audience, the uninformed contemporary reader, or even to the author(s). It is the task of the psychologically trained critic to unfold these dimensions. Adam and Eve are to be considered not as historical figures but as universal representations of male and female. They may potentially signify father, husband, and/or son; mother, wife, and/or daughter. They stand in some relationship to each other—husband-wife, mother-son, father-daughter, brother-sister—and out of these potential relationships the dynamics of the story emerge. Most Freudian interpreters agree that God symbolizes the unconscious father, who creates or gives birth to the son, Adam. However, Eve's part in the drama is much more fluid. While the interpreters agree that she fills the role of mother, they unfold the meaning of this role in differing ways.

Géza Róheim: Incest and Power. Géza Róheim, a hospital psychoanalyst, reads the tale against its ancient Near Eastern background, and in parallel to myths from Europe, Africa, and the Pacific Islands. He examines especially the Babylonian stories of Adapa and Gilgamesh, which he considers to be parallel to Genesis 2–3 (1940). Róheim agrees with the theory that the two trees in Eden were originally only one, and his analysis of Adapa and Gilgamesh leads him to suggest that this earlier form of the paradise story centered on the tree of life alone. The tree of life figures prominently in Babylonian myth and art as representative of the power of the king. It is taboo to any others; taking the fruit of the tree is a usurpation of the king's authority. An attack on the tree or its fruit is an "attack against the father (god, king) himself" (13). Róheim finds confirmation for this dynamic of succession in God's fear that " . . . the man is become like one of us" (Gen 3:22).

The symbol of the tree is ambivalent, however. Alongside the phallic aspect of power and authority appears an additional maternal aspect. The tree bears fruit as a mother bears children; the image of the mother as a vine and children as "the fruit of the womb" is common in the Bible. The characteristic emblem of the Canaanite goddess of fertility, the *ashera* pole, is generally understood to represent a tree. It is not hard to see the tree in Eden as playing a role similar to that of a holy tree, a treasure, or the woman guarded by a serpent or dragon in many hero myths. Róheim describes several versions of a mythic motif of the "Journey to the End of the World," in which a hero travels far away to seek a magical object and overcome (and often slay) a monster or dragon. One of these myths, the Polynesian story of Maui, illustrates what he considers to be essential aspects of the myth. The Journey to the End of the World is a journey of return to the mother; the apples of immortality are the mother's breast. A guardian serpent or dragon symbolizes the sexual anxiety that surrounds the (incestuous) desire to return (in coitus) to the mother. Consequently, it is not surprising that at times the mother (Eve) might herself be identified with the serpent.

Yet Róheim does not consider the paradise story a transparent example of the Journey to the End of the World myth; it has undergone condensation of various mythic motifs that appear only in fragments or hints. According to Freud, condensation is one of the mechanisms by which dream symbols are formed, bringing together elements that ordinarily remain separate in the waking world. Because of this combining, one symbol or element in a dream may represent any number of latent meanings. Therefore, the phallic power aspect of the tree and the motherly, fruit-bearing aspect can coexist within the same symbol. Both, however, point to underlying oedipal dynamics.

The serpent appears as the guardian of the tree, which is the primary locus of phallic power and authority, and as the messenger of the gods. While the present form of the tale intends to depict the serpent as the "villain of the drama," it seems that God has not told the truth about death, while the serpent has. Serpents serve frequently in myth as messengers of the gods. In these myths a striking feature is that often two messengers appear—one aiding life, the other death. Róheim surmises that this duality may be rooted in the early ambivalence of a child toward the parents. An infant's relationship with the mother comprises both a nurturing (life-giving) dimension and an aggressive, incestuous desire, perceived as dangerous or threatening.

The serpent therefore lies symbolically at the nexus of conflicting relationships within the family. As guardian of the tree of life, it is the emblem of the father's power that the son must confront and overcome. It is also identified closely with Eve; Eve's name in Hebrew can mean "serpent." The biblical figure of Eve shows striking similarities to various ancient Near Eastern goddesses often portrayed as serpents or with serpent attendants. Under these two aspects, the serpent recalls two dimensions of the family relations: revolt against the father and sexual attraction to the mother.

Róheim finds it "remarkable" that the very God who grants fertility punishes it. This punishment makes sense only in light of the struggle between son and father. The father grants limited rights to maturity to the son, reserving power to himself. The sin lies not in simply ignoring a prohibition; it is usurpation of what belongs to the father (symbolized by the tree and its fruit) and can only be taken by fighting the father. Róheim cites parallels with the myth of Adapa to advance his theory that "in the latent content of the story of the fall, Adam (Adapa) fought a victorious battle against God the Father (Ea), had intercourse with Eve the Mother and then was afflicted with remorse" (26).

The maternal imagery of the tree contributes further to understanding the sin. If the fruit of the tree symbolizes the breast, the "sin" of eating might be nothing more than the natural infantile need to suckle. Ambivalence and aggression, however, are present even in the earliest stage. The blissful union with the mother in suckling is tinged with aggression, as the child either wants to possess the mother's body or is frustrated by temporary separation from the nipple. A child feels that separation from the mother is punishment for its own aggression. The story asserts that responsibility for the fall, the coming of death, and expulsion from the blissful garden rests with human beings.

Within the oedipal dynamic, incestuous desire for the mother gives rise to the expectation that the father will punish that desire. That punishment may be either objective (from the actual father) or self-inflicted by a father image within the psyche. The punishment, then, is an essential aspect of the story: "Anxiety, shame, an invisible divine voice and punishment then appear in the world; that is: the Oedipus complex is repressed" (26).

Róheim points to Gen 3:20 in which Eve is named as "the mother of all living." This pronouncement is not a punishment; it gives the reason for punishment. Eve is Adam's own mother. Following Levy, Róheim considers the punishment on the serpent ("eating dust") to be a euphemism for coitus. Enmity between the serpent and Eve represents conflict between sexuality and the woman. Pain in childbirth and desire for the male are punishments for intercourse. From the perspective of the superego (introjected father image), sexual desire is disobedience to the father and thus a sin. The punishment is to be doomed to perpetuate the forbidden act.

Finally, Adam's expulsion from the garden is an image of separation from the mother. Adam is now separated from the mother but in death will return to Mother Earth from which he was taken. Róheim also believes that the narrative of Eve's creation has been inverted "by an attempt to prove male superiority" (197). Gen 2:24 had anticipated this theme of separation: a man is separated from his mother in being born and later "cleaves" to his wife as a mother image. This maturing sexuality is experienced as unfortunate since it has torn the man from innocence and childlike pleasure. The penalty for his aggression, conflict, and disobedience in struggling for maturity is to suffer lifelong separation from a longed-for Eden.

Fodor and Jork: Eve as the Phallic Mother. Gudrun Jork, a psychoanalytic student of human development and religious studies, and Israeli psychoanalyst A. Fodor emphasize Eve's identity with the symbolic Earth Mother, placing her in the context of phallic goddesses of the ancient Near East

(Jork 1978; Fodor 1954). As the Earth Mother, Eve symbolizes a particular stage of development of the unconscious image of "mother"—one that undergoes a significant modification within the story. Fodor agrees with Rank's assertion that Eve's creation is a reversal of fact. Out of the original unity of male and female comes a sexual differentiation. The rib, he suggests, is in fact the phallus of the phallic goddess, which is removed or "castrated" and given to Adam. That in the narrative it is Adam, not Eve, who is deprived of a member of the body and that it is not Eve's phallus but a rib "makes no difference to the unconscious" (Fodor 1954:197).

Fodor and Jork make much of Near Eastern serpent goddesses. The combination of Eve and the serpent is a representation of the bisexual mother-goddess, the virgin with a penis. As the projection of the phallic mother, Eve signifies the all-powerful and self-sufficient giver of life. Having both penis and womb and the ability to bear children without losing her virginity, she has the potential for eternal youth. Fodor goes as far as to suggest that Eve's aboriginal form was that of a serpent. As the phallic mother, Eve embodies both of the symbolic dimensions often attributed to the serpent—phallic symbolism and immortality (through shedding the skin). Jork believes that the conflict and outcome of the story arise from Eve's self-sufficiency. As mother-goddess, Eve represents an intolerable threat to the exclusive power of an emergent patriarchal cult of the sky god. As the phallic mother, she is the source not only of life but of all mischief and evil as well.

By identifying Eve with goddesses of the ancient Near East, Fodor and Jork argue that one should read the narrative against the background of conflict between goddess worship and emergent patriarchal god images. This contest mirrors infantile development prior to the oedipal stage. The unconscious contents of the child's relationship with the parents—father and mother—are projected outward and become gods. They suggest that human religious development follows a similar path. In the history of religions the cult of the goddess represents an earlier stage of development. Goddess worship arose out of primitive misunderstanding of the process of procreation. Since the mother gave birth without visible aid from the father, she thus was revered as the source of life. Later, clearer understanding of sexual differentiation and procreation brought forth the image of the bisexual goddess, often depicted as possessing a phallus. This "phallic mother" is an embodiment of infantile fantasies of the omnipotent mother.

According to Fodor and Jork, the next stage of theological development echoes the child's progressive withdrawal from the mother and identification with the father. The replacement of mother by father stirs up ambivalence and guilt in the child, which he or she then projects onto the masculine and feminine god images of myth. The male sky god replaces the self-sufficient bisexual or phallic mother-goddess/Earth Mother.

To account for this shift in religious consciousness they refer to Freud's myth of the murder of the primal father. In his writings, Freud had traced the roots of religion to the incestuous dynamics of the oedipal conflict and to a primal crime of parricide and cannibalism (1955, 1961b, 1964). Building on early evolutionary and anthropological hypotheses, Freud imagined that the earliest social organization of human beings was a primal horde ruled by a tyrannical father who monopolized sexual access to the females. As young males matured and threatened the father's dominance, the father would drive them away or kill them.

At some point in distant prehistory, some exiled brothers banded together, killed the tyrannical father, and ate him. This act reflected their ambivalent relationship to the father because they both feared and envied him. By killing him, they eliminated the threat to themselves; by eating him, they incorporated some part of him into themselves. This ancient "crime" comes to be repeated and commemorated in the totem meal, in which the tribe ritually slaughters and eats a sacred animal.

Freud declares that the totem meal marks the beginning of culture, morality, and religion. Freud surmises that after the murder, the hatred that the sons felt against the domineering father had been satisfied, and their ambivalent affection now emerged as remorse and a sense of guilt. Having internalized the prohibitions previously enforced violently by the father, the sons themselves set limits on each other and themselves. They forbade the killing of the totem animal, which represented the father, and renounced their access to the father's women. These two "fundamental taboos of totemism"—murder and incest—correspond to the repressed wishes of the Oedipus complex, and together they form the earliest basis for religion.

Fodor believes that the sin of Genesis 3 relates to repression of the mother-goddess by patriarchy. He declares that, through serpent symbolism, the story alludes to incestuous love between Adam and Eve. This relationship signifies the dual-unity organization of the infant and the phallic mother, an organization broken up by the father (God). Incest need not necessarily refer to a sexual act—the essence of the incestuous relationship is the unconscious longing to return to the womb, original unity, and absorption. The roots of "original sin" are not to be found in some event in the garden. Rather, it arises from monotheistic ideology, with its effort to restrict and repress longing for the mother.

Jork agrees that the background of the "sin" is oedipal, but reads it in the context of individual psychosexual development. Adam and Eve are placed in a garden and forbidden to eat from the tree of the knowledge of good and evil. The garden presents an image of the fetus in the uterus, since, she suggests, the garden symbolizes the female genitalia. Adam in the garden symbolizes the original state of union with the mother, which may contain several elements: the longed-for dual unity that precedes the initial separation of self and the beloved object (mother), a portrayal of primal human bisexuality before sexual differentiation, and the experience of sexual innocence in early childhood. This longing for return to unity finds expression in Gen 2:24: "and they become one flesh."

The two trees in the garden are phallic symbols of the power and creativity of the father (God). The inclusion of phallic symbols in the midst of the garden—a nurturing, motherly environment—again points to the phallic mother. Furthermore, the tension between the tree of life and the tree of the knowledge of good and evil (which brings death through the transgression of the taboo) call to mind Freud's two basic instincts, the creative and unitive *Eros* and the destructive *Thanatos*.

"Eating" is, as Levy explained, a euphemism for coitus. Eve's eating the fruit signifies incorporation of and identification with what belongs to the father, as in the totem meal as described by Freud. The sin that thus results has several dimensions. It is disobedience to the father, recalling the primordial murder of the horde-father. It represents estrangement from the father and return to union with the mother—historically, a return to tree worship and the forbidden goddess cults, and psychologically, a return to incestuous unity with the mother. Excessive emotional attachment to the mother endangers the process of personality development, for it is ultimately narcissistic; that is, in early development, the child sees the mother as an extension of his or her own self.

The "sin" and its outcome are, however, not entirely negative. For with their eating, the man and woman begin to mature. They become aware of sexual differentiation and realize that they are not perfect and complete. This realization is a blow to the narcissistic ego; their rush to cover their nakedness reveals a need to conceal their imperfection. The search for autonomy, symbolized in union with the mother through eating the fruit, proves futile. They now feel even more vulnerable and dependent and fear punishment by the father (castration anxiety). That castration takes the form of imposed enmity between the serpent and Eve, and her new subjugation to Adam. These represent the castration and dethronement of the phallic mother-goddess. Eve is reduced from a virgin goddess to an earthly mother; the earth she once ruled is now cursed, along with the serpent who had been her attendant.

Simultaneously, the man and woman have taken a step in psychosexual maturity. Psychological development faces serious danger in fixation on symbiosis with the mother; individuals need to separate in order to grow. Guilt and remorse are necessary for moral action. After reality forces the downfall of the Oedipus complex, Adam has now "become like one of us, knowing good and evil" (Gen 3:22). However, patriarchal ideology colors the outcome, which is expressed in the text's linkage of woman, sexuality, and sin. Adam now belongs to the world of the father and, after the expulsion, the patriarchal hierarchy of work and family roles becomes evident. Eve is bound to genital sexuality as punishment while Adam begins the work of civilization and culture. Adam and Eve are finally cast out of the garden; an individual can never return to the original dual unity.

Theodor Reik: The Primal Murder. By far the most thorough Freudian analysis of Genesis 3 was made by Theodor Reik in *Myth and Guilt* (1957). Reik downplays the importance of the incest theme in favor of the fundamental conflict between son and father. He uses a psychoanalytic variation of tradition-criticism to "recover" the earliest form of the story. Eve's connection to the serpent, her similarity to mother-goddesses, and her role as seducer seem to be part of different cycles of myths. Reik believes this indicates that the figures of Eve and the serpent are secondary elaborations. If this is the case, the key figures of the original tale are Adam and God; the original crime cannot have involved sexual transgression. Guilt feelings, common to all human beings, often are connected to sexual desire but can arise from different issues. In this story they seem to have their root in aggression in the oral stage of development, given the central role of "eating."

Expressions like "remorse" (literally "to bite again"), "pangs" of conscience, or "gnawing" guilt seem to reinforce that connection.

The fall story (as Reik designates it) is one example of a common motif in mythology—ancient harmony between God and humanity is broken by some act, intended or accidental, by which people offend God and for which they are punished by expulsion or God's separation from them. Such stories often involve some taboo, such as the forbidden fruit. Reik's question is: What was this original crime?

The symbolism of the tree is key to understanding the story. Reik, like others, considers the two trees to be one. The motif of eating forbidden fruit from the tree appears three times in the story. Why is the fruit forbidden? Because in eating it, Adam "will become like God/one of us" (Gen 3:5, 22). The core story must then be as follows: "Adam ate of a certain tree because he was convinced that meal would make him like God or transform him into a God" (208). Pushing further, Reik calls to mind close associations of the tree of life with the king or god. The tree is a totem, he declares, not merely a symbol for the god, it *is* the god. Genesis 3 tells of someone who ate his god.

Adam's crime is that he ate his god. We find here a veiled retelling of Freud's proposed myth of the murder and eating of the tyrannical horde-father, cloaked in the language of tree totemism. The motive for this rebellious act of cannibalism is the desire to become God and to identify with the father by taking him into one's own body.

Due to the overwhelming horror of this primeval event, Reik claims, human beings repressed its memory. All that remained was a sense of guilt. The original perpetrators had not succeeded; they had not become the father, and now that he was gone they longed for his return. The memory of the father returned in the form of the gods and eventually as the father-god Yahweh, but the memory of his murder remained latent for millennia, known only in a vague sense of guilt. It manifests itself only in concealed form as the sin of eating from the forbidden tree.

Reik goes on to explore how the New Testament understanding of Christ as the "second Adam" relates to the Genesis account. In the centuries leading up to Christ, Reik asserts, an increasing effort to develop and obey the Law leads only to greater guilt. This growing sense of guilt ultimately demands a victim: "The old murder had to be avenged and to be atoned and at the same time to be repeated" (241). Christ's crucifixion revives the memory, still veiled and indirect, but now recognizable. How can a memory return after thousands of years of repression? Reik is vague as to how this might be possible but assumes an analogy between individual and corporate psychologies: "The assumption is that the masses as well as the individual retain impressions of the past in unconscious memory traces that are inaccessible to conscious recollection" (191). The crucifixion corresponds directly to the crime: Christ, the Son of God, is murdered on a cross, which later tradition names the "tree of life." "[I]n the crucifixion Christ is most intimately united with the tree god. Through being hanged on it He becomes one with God Father" (300).

Several points of correspondence between the Christ myth and the fall are confirmation for Reik that his reconstruction of the original "sin" is correct. Primeval man murdered the father, who became the basis for god-images; Jesus is murdered as the son of God. The primeval father was eaten by the sons; Christ's flesh and blood are eaten in the Eucharist. The sons wished to incorporate the father to be like him; Christians seek union with Christ in the Eucharist. The language of the tree totem recalls the act of devouring the father; the cross becomes, like a totem, an object of veneration. Finally, killing and eating the father becomes the original sin; Christ redeems humanity from original sin by offering himself as a sacrifice.

If Adam's transgression had been sexual, Christ's penalty would have required some sexual dimension. Although Genesis 3 does have sexual overtones, these are later interpolations. Part of the motivation for the ancient murder lay in the sons' desire for the father's women. Their remorse for the crime later takes the form of blaming the women for precipitating the act; woman becomes the evil seductress. At the heart of the myth stands the memory of violent murder, cannibalism, and the persistent feeling of guilt arising from them.

COMPARISON AND COMMENT

All these studies share the three key characteristics of Freudian interpretation—equating myth and dream, characteristic methods of symbolic interpretation, and reference to oedipal dynamics. They also evidence both major and minor differences in their development and conclusions. Taken as a whole, rather than offering convergence or agreement, they add to the conflict of interpretations. One wonders whether Róheim's father/daughter and mother/son incest, Fodor's suppression of the phallic mother-goddess, Jork's infantile development, and Reik's primal cannibalism can possibly be found in the same text.

Myth and Dreams

The Freudian interpreters we have examined begin with the assumption that there is continuity, if not identity, between myth symbolism, dream and neurotic imagery, and the manifestations of the personal unconscious. Such close identification of myth and the individual unconscious makes it unclear just what Freudians believe they are studying in this text. Is it the psyche of the author or unconscious dynamics common to all human beings? Their understanding of text collapses the distance between individual and collective and between the past and the present. This assertion that what is historically ancient, what is personally unconscious, what is part of one's childhood experience, and what is primitive in the modern world are all the same has been called the "archaic illusion" (Cunningham 1991:116). Do they mean to assert that, in some sense, the text is a manifestation of the author's own unconscious? If so, the process of analysis becomes an effort to reconstruct the mind of the author. This is not the same hermeneutical assertion that the meaning of the text must accord with the intention of the author; the author's intention is *conscious*, while Freudians concentrate on the *unconscious*. In Freud's theory, the unconscious is always personal; it is the residue of individual experiences, most often from the earliest years of life, which are repressed and concealed from the conscious mind.

None of the critics we have examined, however, claim to be analyzing the author. Instead, they read the symbolism of Genesis 3 as though humanity itself were an individual in analysis. They interpret change through history as if it were the psychic growth of humanity. Thus, for example, Jork and Fodor posit that in the history of religions, patriarchal/ father religions develop out of more "primitive" mother/goddess religions. Reik's assertion that a primal father-murder, repressed in human consciousness for millennia, suddenly re-emerges depends entirely on the assumption that collective human development exactly parallels that of the individual, as understood in Freudian terms.

Symbolic Language

Dream and mythic images, these Freudians assert, can undergo all manner of transformation on their way to becoming manifest. The unconscious always expresses itself in distorted and concealed ways, and thus one requires a hermeneutic of suspicion to decipher the otherwise opaque symbolism of the text. The present form of the text is highly suspect; mythic and dream symbols modify and conceal the "true" meaning of the unconscious by a variety of means, including substitution, displacement, condensation, conversion, and inversion. In the practice of psychotherapy, the actual patient on the couch exercises some measure of control. Without such control, however, the mechanisms of Freudian dream interpretation may deliver a bag of tools able to convert *any* text into the desired form. The text itself cannot control interpretation; it is already suspect.

Interpretation under Freudian auspices thus presents significant problems and challenges for conventional exegesis. Symbols are quite fluid. One can interpret symbols as substituting for something else, as merging two or more referents, as splitting one referent into two or more symbols, or inverting the significance entirely. This fluidity accounts not only for much of the conflict among the different interpretations but for inconsistencies within individual analyses. Levy, for example, can identify the fruit both with apples and figs. Rank inverts the narrative of Genesis 2, presenting Eve as both the wife and daughter of God. Róheim can assert both phallic and maternal meanings for the tree, and Fodor can say that it is unimportant to the unconscious whether Adam loses a rib or Eve a phallus.

While Freud himself cautioned against a "cipher method," in which the meaning of dream elements are fixed and can be looked up in a "dream book," his followers employ methods that seem not far distant from just that. They identify symbolic elements (serpent, tree, etc.), often taken in isolation, declare them to be "incestuous" symbols, and having made that association, summon examples from other myths to buttress their case. Even Levy, who asserts that the symbolism is largely conscious, compares isolated figures like the fruit (which he variously identifies with apples, pomegranates, and figs) with similar items in *Faust*, Greek and Roman mythology, Palestinian love songs, Voltaire's poetry, and French slang, and considers them all to be identical. Rank is convinced that the serpent can only be a symbol of incest and shows that the serpent is a common motif in myths of incest and also appears in the neurotic fantasies of patients in incestuous situations. He assumes that there is continuity among all these manifestations but must suggest different (conflicting) references for it. It may represent Adam, who commits incest with his mother, Eve. Or it may denote God, since the serpent is connected to father-daughter incest. By inversion, it may also represent the jealous God protecting his daughter from incest. The consequence of wrenching these elements out of their specific context and reducing them to a common set of "meanings" is that these critics ultimately homogenize the richness of diverse mythologies and reduce them to a limited set of possibilities.

Dream symbols, however, are overdetermined—they arise out of multiple, even contradictory, unconscious factors. Multiple interpretations are not merely possible; they are essential. In the therapeutic situation, the dreamer's personal history, further dreams, and fantasies play the role of validation of any given interpretations, associations, and responses. Here, however, we have no dreamer, no one to develop and clarify the story's significance. Other mythic material may serve to validate an analysis, but can we be sure that such material is truly from the same "dreamer"? Furthermore, mythic material is not primary dream or fantasy; it has been selected, reshaped, edited, and transmitted through different cultures and traditions. Myths are already *interpreted* myth.

Oedipal Dynamics

With such latitude in symbolic interpretation, the presuppositions of the interpreter clearly play a major role in Freudian analysis. Without the verification of an individual analysand, a critic's choice of "parallel" material affects the interpretation significantly. Because Freudian interpretation collapses distinctions of past and present, individual and collective, analysts frequently ignore differences of culture, history, and social context in finding examples to support their arguments.

Having made the initial identification between the story and the functions of the unconscious, Freudians are less interested in interpreting the text as a whole than in the application of theory, most specifically that of the Oedipus complex. Since the unconscious acts deceptively in manifesting itself, one must be highly suspicious of the present form of the text. The key task, then, is to delve back into the world behind the text to recover the original or archaic form of the story. Their efforts to do so recall Freud's own self-confessed "autocratic and arbitrary" use of biblical tradition. Each interpreter, depending on the sources he or she has invoked as parallels and on the mechanisms they see at work in the distortion of the story, argues for a different "original" or fills out the basic framework in differing ways. One is left with the inescapable impression that these interpreters have often reasoned backward from their conclusions to arrive at their proposed "original" text.

Rank's suggestion that the Eden narrative contains a significant inversion (Eve born from Adam, rather than the *true* situation) provides the linchpin for interpreting the story in terms of incest and the Oedipus complex. As Freud himself remarked, "Then everything would be clear; Eve would be Adam's mother, and we should be dealing with the well-known motif of mother incest, the punishment for which, etc." (quoted by McGuire 1974:473). Among Freudians, the conflict of interpretations takes the form of differing arguments as to just *how* the story evidences incestual motifs more than *whether* that is the case. A second significant inversion, unrecognized by the biblical critics, is necessary to fit the story into the oedipal framework. Genesis 3 becomes a story about the *man*—*his* desire for his mother, *his* struggle with the father God, *his* disobedience of the command. The woman, who in the story speaks and acts decisively, becomes nothing more than a pawn in an incestual game.

The hermeneutic circle can take a seemingly closed form in Freudian exegeses. Seizing on just a few of the story's symbols and highlighting portions of their potential significance, the writers consider these symbols to be the "same" as those found in a selected group of incestuous myths. Beyond comparing the overall themes of such stories for the insight they might provide into the dynamics of rebellion and guilt, they argue that individual details must correspond exactly to each other. They illuminate Genesis by means of tales that may have only tangential similarity to it, such as the Oedipus myth itself or other myths from Greek, African, or Polynesian sources. They declare that the symbolic elements in these parallels are "incestuous" without offering supporting evidence. Further, they tend to concretize metaphorical use of incest symbols into actual acts (or desires) of incest. An unspoken canon of incest stories (both mythic and clinical) seems to serve in Freudian circles as reinforcement for symbolic interpretation. Criteria for inclusion in this canon are not historical, cultural, or even literary; the critics assume that materials are parallel because they share some symbolic elements and, to a lesser extent, certain interactions between the figures. These early Freudians often appear not to be exegeting Genesis 3 but oedipal literature, insisting, based on their reconstructions, that Genesis 3 belongs in this category.

The challenge to conventional biblical interpretation leveled by Freudian interpretation is for exegetes to recognize that many aspects of texts go beyond rational, historical, and literary categories. One requires special sensitivity and hermeneutical techniques to penetrate the "false consciousness" of surface interpretations. The particular weakness of psychoanalytic criticism is largely a function of using a helpful tool for the wrong task. Whether because they were constrained by the historical-critical model of biblical interpretation that was dominant in their day or caught in their own historical problem of identifying individual and collective psyches, Freudians without exception understood their work to be the recovery of the (un)consciousness that lies *behind* the text. However, while biblical scholars have rejected Freudian analysis in the main, it nonetheless has made inroads into biblical studies through such methodologies as deconstruction, which takes seriously the Freudian challenge to the transparency of language and interpretation. In *Freud and Philosophy*, Ricoeur began to explore the implications of Freud for a critique of consciousness and language, and critics such as Lacan, Derrida, Irigaray, and Kristeva, who have all had notable influence on biblical studies, have all developed that theme (Aichele et al. 1995).

CRITERIA OF ADEQUACY

How do these readings measure up to our proposed criteria of adequacy? Except for Reik, none of these interpreters deals well with the chapter as a whole. For the most part, each centers on the sexual/familial relationships of Adam and Eve and develops those implications to the exclusion of any other themes. In so doing, they rely on inversions of the manifest text. Displaying what at times approaches disdain for the text as it stands, Freudian interpreters may not be reading the same text; they are intent on "recovering" or "reconstructing" some more archaic or "purer" version of the tale. Even Reik, who analyzes the Eden story quite thoroughly, accounting not only for his "recovered" text but also for New Testament references to it, discards the major part of the canonical text.

Neither are these exegetes very successful at dealing with the uniqueness of the story. In their concern to find parallels within a broad range of human traditions and rituals, they gloss over (or argue against) unique details in the text. The authors read their parallels quite selectively, passing over aspects that do not suit their point.

Since most of our writers are concerned to highlight only the unconscious dynamics at work in the text, they do not attempt to account for every factor. They consider it sufficient to declare that the current form of the narrative is attributable to either unconscious "repression" or conscious "tradition." Even with respect to the factors with which they do deal, our analysts feel no overwhelming need to seek agreement or convergence. Following lines of argument within any one study is often difficult. In part this is due to the bewildering spectrum of "parallel" material of different kinds from widely varying cultures and periods and to the fluidity of symbolic interpretation.

The Freudians ignore significant elements of the text completely. All understand the story to be primarily about Adam, although Eve is the principal actor in the narrative. They have reduced Eve to an object of incestuous desire and/or action. Not one exegete attempts to interpret the dialogue between Eve and the serpent (which takes up one-fifth of the verses in chapter 3).

Freudian interpretation does enable the text to mean all it can mean, in that it considers aspects of the text omitted in conventional exegesis. Using a Freudian hermeneutic of suspicion highlights unconscious dimensions of the text that no other method can uncover. On the other hand, one can find a definite tendency toward reductionism—contending that the story is "nothing more" than its latent meaning; all other possible interpretations are valid only as clues to the unconscious meaning. Those who do not accept Freudian models of the psyche and human development will contend that such readings are pure eisegesis; our interpreters claim rather that they illuminate otherwise obscure aspects of the text.

Does Freudian analysis move the reader toward appropriation? For one who accepts the Freudian framework, these studies make the story intelligible. Yet the underlying purpose of all the critics seems not so much to unfold the story as to enlist it as yet another proof of the validity of Freudian theory. Rather than seeking to unfold the world of the text so that the reader can engage it and be engaged by it, they seem more interested in fitting the text into the world of Freudian thought.

In relation to Ricoeur's further criteria for psychoanalytic interpretation, these works are more effective. Each is coherent in its own way with

Freudian theory, although each emphasizes different aspects of that theory. The fundamental question remains about how well that theory accords with fact. For example, Reik's analysis builds brilliantly on Freud's "scientific myth" of the primal horde, but that myth itself is deeply flawed. In the same way, each analysis uses accepted rules for decoding unconscious phenomena, but the question remains whether assuming that myths are in every way analogous to dreams is legitimate.

Assessing the therapeutic adequacy of such efforts is more difficult. Since no "analysand" exists as such, how does a Freudian unfolding of the text aid in working through unconscious issues? Whom does it benefit: The interpreter? The reader? Humanity as a whole? Finally, each author has attempted to sketch a comprehensible "story behind the story" in deciphering the symbols of the text. While they have been relatively successful within the framework of Freudian theory, the very nature of that theory and the elasticity of interpretive method make it difficult for such explanations to be intelligible beyond the Freudian circle.

5
"Utterances of the Soul": Jung and Analytical Psychology

We must read the Bible or we shall not understand psychology. Our psychology, our whole lives, our language and imagery are built upon the Bible.

—Jung 1976:156

I would go a step further and say that the statements made in the Holy Scriptures are also utterances of the soul . . . they point to realities that transcend consciousness. These entia *are the archetypes of the collective unconscious, and they precipitate complexes of ideas in the form of mythological motifs.*

—Jung 1952:557

It is evident from these two comments that Carl G. Jung held the Bible in higher esteem than did Freud. Indeed, Jung's writings are replete with direct and indirect references to biblical texts, allusions to biblical personages, places, symbols, and biblical phrases and concepts. Ten pages of the general index to Jung's *Collected Works* are devoted to biblical citations alone, not including additional allusions to biblical persons, stories, symbols, and theology. Whether it is true that one cannot understand psychology without reading the Bible, it is true that one cannot otherwise understand Jung. Jung's immediate and extended family included several clergy, and his childhood immersion in a world of theological debate and biblical texts is evidenced both explicitly and implicitly throughout his writings.

By describing Scripture as the "utterances of the soul," Jung meant that biblical texts symbolically express profound truths that have their origin in the unconscious. Two aspects of Jung's theory and practice provide a key for understanding Jungian biblical hermeneutics: the ideas of archetypes and individuation. Less central, yet still significant as a working assumption, is the technique of amplification.

ARCHETYPES AND THE PSYCHE

In Jung's view, the human psyche comprises several interrelated elements. Consciousness is that part of our psyches that we experience directly. Our sense perceptions of the world around us and our recognition, evaluation, and interpretation of them are the contents of the conscious mind. This cluster of perceptions, experiences, values, and choices—those things that I call "myself"—is organized and shaped by a "virtual center," the ego.

Along with Freud, Jung recognized the reality of the unconscious. The personal unconscious contains "lost memories, painful ideas that are repressed (that is, forgotten on purpose), subliminal perceptions, by which are meant sense perceptions that were not strong enough to reach consciousness, and finally, contents that are not ripe for consciousness" (1966b:103). It is, as the name implies, the repository of material from the personal experience of the individual.

Unlike Freud, however, Jung believed other psychic phenomena cannot be explained based on a purely personal unconscious. Jung cites hundreds of examples of his patients who experienced, in dreams and delusions, images and symbols that expressed mythic motifs with which they could not have come into contact. These manifestations led Jung to suggest a deeper and more universal level of the unconscious, which he named the "collective unconscious."

The collective unconscious, he declared, is inherited, not developed, and is universal and impersonal. A "world of images," "the collective unconscious—so far as we can say anything about it at all—appears to consist of mythological motifs or primordial images." These "images," or more properly, the source that generates these images, Jung called "archetypes." Archetypes are not derived from the individual's experience but are patterning structures of the psyche, without specific content until the unique experience of the individual brings them forth. Archetypes are unknowable in themselves but are projected in dream images, fantasies, and myth. Biblical stories quite often express unconscious projections of psychic archetypes.

This projection of archetypes into myths and stories provides the theoretical basis for Jungian literary criticism. Even when a story shows no concern for "psychological" issues (as biblical stories do not), the collective patterning and projecting processes are still operating. In fact, as Jung remarked about modern literature, "in general, it is the non-psychological novel [in contrast to the 'psychological novel'] that offers the richest opportunities . . . such a tale is constructed against a background of unspoken psychological assumptions, and the more unconscious the author is of them, the more this background reveals itself . . . " (1966a:137). Although they are the source of myth and symbols, archetypes are not to be identified with specific mythological images or motifs; they are solely "the tendency to form such representations of a motif—representations that can vary a great deal in detail without losing their basic pattern" (1961:67).

Jung identified several archetypes, including among others the shadow, the anima/animus, and the Self. The shadow has both personal and collective dimensions. Personally, it encompasses aspects of a person that the conscious ego has rejected, underdeveloped, and undervalued. Collectively, it contains the totality of what society denies, rejects, or considers "evil." The shadow is often projected onto others, or appears in dreams and myths as a dark, threatening figure.

The anima (in men; for women the corresponding archetype is the animus) is the contrasexual dimension of the psyche, shaped by the individual's personal experience of the opposite sex, by the man's own femininity (or the woman's masculinity), and by inherited collective images. The final comprehensive archetype is the Self. Present from the very beginning as the unconscious possibility of wholeness, the Self is both the guiding principle and the final goal of the total personality. It is "the completest expression of that fateful combination we call individuality," encompassing both conscious and unconscious elements (1966b:404). As a guide, the Self is the source of the inner drive to psychic growth, the sender of dreams, and a regulating center. The Self is expressed in images and symbols of totality, especially religious ones. The Christ, the Buddha, the "Son of Man," and the "Adam Kadmon" (second Adam) of kabbalah and alchemy share this dimension of the "total human being" (1961:202). One often experiences an encounter with the Self as a meeting with the divine.

Individuation

It is essential for psychological growth and maturity that an individual recognizes and relates to the archetypes, a process Jung called "individuation." "Individuation means becoming an 'in-dividual', and, in so far as 'individuality' embraces our innermost, last, and incomparable uniqueness, it also implies becoming one's own self. We could therefore translate individuation as 'coming to selfhood' or 'self-realization.'" (1966b:266). Individuation is the process of psychic development within the individual. It begins with the task of developing the conscious ego, which emerges out of unconscious identification with the world into self-awareness and separation. In later life, individuation involves relating to and assimilating the unconscious dimensions of the personality—the archetypes of the shadow, the animus/anima and the Self—in unfolding the unique individuality of the person.

Amplification and Active Imagination

Since archetypes cannot be known directly but are expressed in symbols, dreams, and mythic images, careful exploration of these manifestations is necessary to clarify and reveal what lies behind them. In Jungian analytical practice two key methods for this task are amplification and active imagination. Amplification involves the expansion of (dream) symbols through association with similar material, both personal and collective, in order to clarify underlying significances. Amplification is founded on the assertion that the archetypal source of mythic or dream symbols is universal to humankind, despite cultural or historical contexts. Thus, Jungian interpreters, like Freudians, will often draw on "parallel" myths to illuminate important details.

Jung's attitude toward myth, however, is quite different from Freud's. Freud considered the manifest form of dreams and myths to be the result of an unconscious desire to conceal and distort the latent contents of the unconscious. Comparison to other mythic material, for Freud, is a way to strip away the deceptive façade and unearth the real significance of the myth. Jung, on the other hand, considers symbols to be more expressive than repressive. The task is not to reduce symbols to some core signification; it is rather to expand, enrich, and elucidate them by invoking other examples of archetypal expression.

The technique of active imagination, highly significant in the therapeutic setting, plays very little role in more formal critical studies. Active imagination involves concentrating on a symbol or image until it begins to develop in the imagination, to gain in detail and movement. The conscious mind does not control active imagination; rather, images emerge according to their own structure and unfold a life of their own. It allows an individual to engage the symbol more fully by allowing the archetypal foundation of the symbol to unfold itself in present experience. It is "to dream the myth onwards and give it a modern dress" (1968:271). Because active imagination is essentially both unconscious (though the "active" part involves conscious relatedness) and personal, it does not fit easily into conventional biblical interpretation.

JUNG AND GENESIS 3

For all the wealth of biblical material in his writings, Jung did not concern himself with biblical commentary per se. He was, after all, a psychologist and not a biblical scholar or theologian. In the introduction to *Answer to Job,* his only extended scriptural treatment, he writes, "I do not write as a biblical scholar (which I am not), but as a layman and a physician who has been privileged to see deeply into the psychic life of many people" (1952:559). His biblical allusions serve as illustrations of his theories, not as primary material for analysis. Thus, Jung nowhere embarks on a systematic analysis of Genesis 3. Just as with Freud, however, his comments on the text hint at themes that his followers will later develop.

Jung's attention in the first chapters of Genesis is drawn primarily to the figures of Adam and Eve. His development of these figures, however, is related more closely to their representation in medieval alchemy than to the biblical characters. Jung considered alchemical imagery to be expressive of the dynamics of psychic development. Alchemy was, for Jung, the outward projection of what were, in fact, inner processes. Thus, much of what Jung has to say about Adam and Eve is not the result of his reading of Genesis; it is Jung's reading of the alchemists' reading of Genesis.

According to Jung, Adam's initial state is a representation of the whole psyche. Adam is androgynous, comprising both male and female (animus and anima), and unites several opposites in his dual nature: light and dark, godly and earthly, physical and spiritual. Created in the image of God, he is a symbol of the Self, a visualization of the "irrepresentable Godhead" (1968:558). Eve subsequently emerges out of Adam as the embodiment of his anima, or soul. The soul is that which indiscriminately seeks life, without regard to conventional moral categories. Eve, then, "could not rest content until she had convinced Adam of the goodness of the forbidden apple" (1968:56).

Garden, Serpent, and Tree

Christian iconography often depicts the garden into which the man and woman are placed as a mandala—a symmetrical (usually circular) image divided into geometric patterns. The mandala, which often appears spontaneously in dream images and artwork during psychotherapy, is a representation of the totality of consciousness and is in Jungian theory an important symbol of the process of individuation. The Garden of Eden is the image of total harmony and totality, containing the four rivers that encompass the whole world.

Jung does not deal consistently or extensively with the trees at the center of the garden. The tree of life, he notes, is the same archetypal image as the "Philosophical Tree" in alchemy, where, he contends, it is also an image of individuation. In other cultures the tree of life is often a mother symbol, and the combination of the tree and serpent is a symbol of the mother protected against incest, but Jung does not develop this aspect further in relation to the tree in Eden.

The serpent gets more attention. Serpents are common images in dreams and mythology and can represent different unconscious archetypes. They may personify the spirit of the mother-tree just as the serpent in Genesis functions as the "voice" of the tree. Artworks depicting the temptation often portray the serpent as feminine; as such, the serpent represents the anima in her aspect as the totality of unconscious contents. More specifically, the serpent personifies the shadow—the vulnerable, weak, and unconscious dimensions of the personality. As the collective unconscious, the serpent "seems to possess a peculiar wisdom of its own and a knowledge that is often felt to be supernatural." This wisdom and knowledge are the "treasure" guarded by the serpent or dragon and explain the dual aspect of the serpent as guardian of wisdom and tempter or destroyer. "Its unrelatedness, coldness, and dangerousness express the instinctuality that with ruthless cruelty rides roughshod over all moral and any other human wishes and considerations and is therefore just as terrifying and fascinating in its effects as the sudden glance of a poisonous snake"

(1968:370). The aspect of the serpent that Jung finds most intriguing is the fact that God created it and placed it in the garden. The blame for the fall must be placed at the feet of God, not humanity.

The Fall and Consciousness

Above all, Jung declares, Genesis 3 is the story of the birth of human consciousness. "The knowledge of good and evil" is conscious self-awareness, the ability to make distinctions. When a child first begins to distinguish some element of its world—when she "knows" someone or something—we say she has consciousness. However, this knowledge appears as an intrusion into the divine realm ("you will be like God, knowing good and evil"). This intrusion, as in the myth of Prometheus, carries with it the danger of inflation. Inflation is an exaggerated sense of self-importance, which often follows a step into wider consciousness. It is because of the danger of inflation that Genesis represents eating the fruit of knowledge as "a deadly sin." In becoming conscious, Adam and Eve broke the original unity of creation, and, by necessity, had to sacrifice their former childlike unconscious union. They experience this fragmentation, separation, and awareness of individuality as death, disobedience, and sin. It is a "Luciferian deed" (1967:415).

Still, it is a necessary deed if one is to become fully human. Jung finds hints that God, in fact, willed the fall. God created the serpent; God made sure that Adam knew where the tree was before forbidding it. Perhaps one can learn something important from this human drive toward consciousness, despite the consequences. Indeed, the church expressed this paradox in the doctrine of the "happy fault" (*felix culpa*)—the recognition that without the disobedience of Adam and Eve, the redemption of the world would not have been possible.

Several critics have followed Jung's lead and have elaborated his initial insights into Genesis 3. John Sanford, Edward Edinger, Mario Jacoby, and Heinz Westman each proposed extensive interpretations of the text. Jolanda Jacobi, Frances Landy, and Rivkah Schärf Kluger have highlighted specific aspects. Jo Milgrom offers a unique approach to the text in what she calls "handmade midrash," a form of amplification.

John Sanford: In Defense of Adam and Eve. John Sanford, a Jungian analyst and Episcopal priest, developed a clear and complete Jungian analysis of Genesis 3, synthesizing many of Jung's own observations into a coherent whole (1981). A myth such as that of Adam and Eve, Sanford explains, contains what one might call "the language of the archetypes"—a narrative representation of unconscious patterns that are universal in human development. Any interpretation of the myth must attend to all the details of the story. An interpretation that omits portions of the myth must be called into question.

Adam is a being comprising pairs of opposites: "matter and spirit, earth and heaven, the mortal and the Divine" (115). This being is set into the Garden of Eden, which has the form of a mandala: the trees mark its central point, the rivers flow from it; everything suggests balance and completeness. The tree of life is familiar as the cosmic tree that appears in many myths, marking the intersection of earth and heaven. Adam's androgyny reflects the animus/anima pattern: all human beings contain masculine and feminine aspects, a theme that is found in myths throughout the world. In Eve, Adam finds the personification of his "other half"; Sanford writes, "the psychic image behind sexual desire is the yearning for wholeness" (117).

Eve's sin is not so much disobedience as it is *curiosity*, a desire to know, and to have the power that knowledge confers. In eating, she and Adam have their eyes opened—they come to consciousness. It is, however, a painful consciousness: they become aware of their sexuality and nakedness and experience shame. When God discovers what they have done, God punishes them and the serpent and expels Adam and Eve from the garden.

Traditional interpretations of the story fail to account for several key questions that the story raises. The punishments seem too harsh and do not appear to fit the crime; the entire situation looks like a set-up. Why had God placed the serpent in the garden? Why give the human beings freedom of choice if God's ultimate purpose was to maintain an eternal paradise? As Sanford puts it, "For God to create curious beings like the first man and woman, place them in a garden with the gift of free will, point out to them this miraculous fruit, goad their curiosity by placing a tempting serpent with them, go off and leave them alone, and then be surprised at what they did and make a big deal about it, is an interpretation which surely does not do justice to this subtle tale" (122).

Sanford calls to mind the alternate interpretation of the story held by some Gnostics, in which the serpent represents the wise deliverer who rescues Adam and Eve from the evil God who wishes to keep them enslaved.

He further considers the story of Prometheus, who steals fire from the gods to give it to humanity. Both these stories highlight the gift of consciousness. Is not the key to understanding Genesis 3 the recognition that Adam and Eve have gained consciousness—a self-reflective ego?

In this light, the events of the story are no mistake; everything aims at precisely this desired outcome. We can see the serpent, created by God, as a personification of the inner drive for psychological development within the human. Without this crucial step into consciousness, Adam and Eve could not lead morally or spiritually meaningful lives. Moral growth can only take place in a world of genuine conflict and choice. Consciousness stands at the beginning of spiritual development, but it also drives the individual out of unconscious identification with nature, with no chance of return.

The dawning of consciousness is something that must have happened at some point in the evolution of humanity, setting human beings apart from the animals. Yet it is also something that happens for each individual. As the ego is formed, and one develops self-consciousness, one also comes to know the tensions of good and evil and a sense of guilt. Guilt is not learned; it is inherent in consciousness itself.

Sanford concludes his reading with a reference to the idea of the "happy fault" (*felix culpa*), which he attributes to Gregory of Nyssa (330–395). It was better, Gregory felt, that humanity had taken the path of knowing good and evil, for this made possible a deeper relationship with God. This view makes good psychological sense, for the story of Adam and Eve describes the beginning of individuation, a development of the psyche that involves suffering, loss, and moral struggle, but also holds the potential of wholeness.

Edward Edinger: Individuation Symbolism. Edward Edinger is a Jungian analyst who has written extensively on religious themes. He first proposed a Jungian reading of Genesis in *Ego and Archetype* (1972) and then returned to the text in his later works *Anatomy of the Psyche* (1985) and *The Bible and the Psyche* (1986). His primary concern is the process of individuation, as the individual psyche moves from identification with the ego (subjective identity) to relationship with the Self (objective identity). While Jung had studied individuation in the later half of life, others have attempted to trace its early developmental stages. Erich Neumann, for example, borrowed an image from Greek mythology, the serpent devouring its own tail, to describe primordial ego-Self identity. Out of this circle of unconscious absorption the ego is born (1954). Increasing separation of the ego from the Self is the primary task of individuation in the first half of life; in the second half, the ego must reunite with the Self through consciousness.

In its original identification with the Self, the ego suffers from inflation, an illusion of self-sufficiency and completion characteristic of young children. As it begins to separate from the Self, the ego experiences deflation. Thus, we traditionally call the Genesis story the fall. The story begins with primordial unity: the garden is a mandala, an image of the Self, and Adam is hermaphroditic, symbolizing wholeness. Adam's creation from earth and breath involves a union of opposites—matter and spirit—but "with an emphasis on matter, since his very name means earth" (Edinger 1986:270).

The serpent's approach is an appeal to inflation. His appeal is to Eve's desire "to be like God." With their decision to act out their inflation, Adam and Eve embark on the path of awareness. The fruit grants them the knowledge of good and evil, the ability to distinguish between opposites, which is the essence of consciousness. To gain consciousness appears in the tale (and subsequent theological interpretation) as a crime against God, the original sin of arrogant pride. By contrast, Edinger points to the contrasting gnostic interpretation that the serpent is the bringer of wisdom and redemption from bondage. This view accords with the psychological interpretation. The serpent's action "represents the urge to self-realization . . . and symbolizes the principle of individuation" (1972:18).

Eating the forbidden fruit propels Adam and Eve from original identification into a world of alienation, suffering, and conflict. It is no surprise that people resist moving into consciousness. They become aware of their nakedness and instinctual feelings are met with shame, taboo, and repression. Newly born consciousness must resist the unconscious in order to maintain its own existence.

Only then does the other tree in the garden, the tree of life, emerge into the foreground. According to a later Jewish tradition, the tree of knowledge forms a hedge around the tree of life. One can only approach the tree of life by way of knowledge and consciousness.

From his work with dream imagery, Edinger notes that dreams that appear during times of individuation often display the motifs of the Genesis story. One dreams of meeting or being bitten by a snake or of having committed a crime. One experiences each new stage of psychological development as a violation of the earlier stage and carries with it a sense of crime and guilt. On the other hand, dreams that involve the offer of something to eat generally signify that some unconscious content is ready to be assimilated by the ego.

Edinger finds a parallel to the Genesis tale in the Greek myth of Prometheus. In both stories, the gods withhold the symbols of consciousness (fire and the knowledge of good and evil). Prometheus steals the fire as Adam and Eve take the fruit. Punishment follows: Prometheus is chained to the rock while daily a vulture tears his liver out, and Adam and Eve suffer pain and toil and expulsion from the garden. Both stories refer to the necessary consequence of consciousness. Pain and suffering certainly exist in the world prior to one's experience of them, but without consciousness, "they do not exist psychologically" (1972:25).

Both stories express the archetypal reality that the development of the psyche requires an inflated act of arrogant pride (hubris) against the Self. Without such a "crime," the psyche is blocked; it cannot proceed. When one takes a step forward, one experiences it not only as a crime against the "powers that be" but as an offense against the collective. The individual's identification with collective groups and institutions like church, family, or nation changes and may seem to others in the group like a betrayal or assault.

Mario Jacoby: The Archetype of Paradise. Mario Jacoby's point of departure for his work *Longing for Paradise* is a clinical concern for patients caught up in the archetype that manifests itself in images of paradise and utopia (1985). In the second part of his book, Jacoby undertakes an extensive psychological interpretation of the biblical text. He begins with the case history of an analysand whose dreams and fantasies contain images closely related to the biblical paradise.

The patient's desire for a "predestined partner" reminds Jacoby of Gen 2:21-22 ("bone of my bones and flesh of my flesh"). One might interpret this text as a description of a "narcissistic object relationship"—a relationship in which a man projects his anima onto a woman so that she becomes for him nothing more than the fulfillment of an inner fantasy. Jacoby notes that readers have often used the text to support the idea of the inferiority of women, and that there are definite patriarchal overtones to the Genesis story. Ultimately, he suggests, it is perhaps most appropriate to say that creation myths—which are always about the dawning of consciousness—require the evolution of pairs of opposites out of original unity. "From the unity of one there comes at first two-in-unity, until the 'Fall' creates polarity" (111).

Jacoby briefly surveys modern criticism of the text, noting its multiple sources, its borrowing of mythic motifs of the ancient Near East, and its theological rewriting of mythic material. Psychologically, he concludes, the story is self-consistent; whether or not it is myth, strictly speaking, it is a legitimate elaboration of a mythological statement. The evidence for this fact lies in its continuing impact on generations of readers and interpreters. The human fascination with the story points to some archetypal dimension that we can never fully unravel.

Interpretations by Philo, the church fathers, and finally Augustine lead Jacoby to consider what "original sin" means in psychological terms. Guilt is integral to the condition of living within human limitations in that we will always cause pain to others, however unintentionally. However, guilt cannot arise without consciousness, since "paradise" represents a life free from guilt but also a life of childish innocence. Guilt begins only with conscience, the awareness of the consequences of one's actions. This awareness begins with doubt—questioning the way things are. Thus, Eve takes the first steps toward the fall when the serpent leads her to question God's commandment. The serpent stands as a symbol of the human capacity for doubt. It is ambivalent. To established order, doubt is evil and threatening, but in the continual changes of life, doubt can be necessary. Doubt can clear the way for a new orientation to reality.

This doubt is essential for the normal development of conscience. When it is met with an empathic mother figure, one who remains caring and present despite the "hurt," the child learns to accept the ambivalence of human life and to take responsibility. Such a mother enables the child to develop a sense of inner order and a conscience that "sounds the alarm whenever the intentions of ego-consciousness deviate too far from the primal order of human existence (the *Self*, in the Jungian sense of the word)." If the mother is not adequate, the child develops a deep-seated and undefined sense of guilt without the possibility of redemption. This pathological guilt, he suggests, is the root of obsessive behavior. The individual constantly attempts to atone for an undefined "sin," motivated by an unavoidable sense of guilt.

The God of paradise evidences an ordering presence like the empathetic mother. We can understand this God, Jacoby argues, as "the ordering factor, the principle of structure in nature, more or less as the center of natural, biopsychic regulation." The Garden of Eden, the place of unity, growth, and abundance, portrays the archetype of the Great Mother. Spirit and nature are undivided; all is bound up in the unconscious union that Jung termed "absolute knowledge"—life's self-regulation. The call of God, "Where are you?" comes to Adam and Eve when the polarity of good and evil has come to awareness and the unity has been shattered. One consequence of this disruption is that human consciousness cannot fully participate in what is timeless and eternal and thus cannot approach the tree of life.

The process of development of the conscience evokes yet another archetype, that of the Father. With the loss of original unity comes a need for external norms and standards to guide the developing conscience. Such guidelines help to order communal life and are learned from relationships to the collective. There is, however, a dimension of conscience that cannot be identified with received collective values, and at times conscience leads an individual to go against established norms. The internalization of norms is not an automatic process but a highly complex development over many years. This dimension of self-judgment by internalized standards is part of the experience called "original sin." Another dimension of "original sin" can be described in terms of Jung's notion of the shadow—just as light creates a conventional shadow, the light of consciousness gives the psychic shadow its shape. That is, whatever is not admitted into consciousness remains in the shadow, and thus the shadow differs from individual to individual. It is not necessarily evil but includes what is simply unknown, unclear, or undervalued.

The danger of the shadow is that one will project it onto others. One attributes qualities to another that properly are one's own, and responds to those projected aspects with hostility. What is required is to recognize the projection and take ownership of the shadow elements. Jacoby suggests that what we call "original sin" is very nearly what we experience with the shadow. Common to all humanity, it contaminates our relationships and good intentions. However, rather than rejecting the shadow, we must engage it and transform it into consciousness.

The Genesis story is not very positive about the realities of human life after the awakening of consciousness. Suffering follows immediately in the form of curses on the serpent and the earth, and the pains of the woman and man. Hostility between the woman and serpent expresses the conflict between consciousness and instinct, "spirit" and "flesh." The instinctive serpent is diminished ("on your belly you shall go"). Yet instinct remains unconsciously at hand, ready to exploit human disunity. Eve will now bear children in pain. She had given birth to nothing in paradise; new life in the world means entering the reality of birth and death, the need for continual renewal. Pain is often characteristic of human development toward maturity and is often essential for transformation. Conscious humanity becomes the worker and maker. Humanity's self-divided nature makes the fruits of culture ambiguous; civilization brings both possibility and destruction.

Finally, the gates to Eden are blocked. No return to paradise is possible. To seek a blissful paradise requires blindness to some aspect of the real situation; humanity's eyes have been opened. Paradise cannot be consciously realized. The longing for paradise remains active in the psyche, often as a desire for happiness, or a wish to avoid tension and anxiety. Nevertheless, "the great lesson of 'post-paradisial existence'" is "to learn and accept the fact that the human state of being-in-conflict is actually necessary for the development of consciousness and maturity" (178).

Heinz Westman: The Springs of Creativity. Analyst Heinz Westman asserts that the Bible delineates "a reliable natural history of man's progress through the inner world . . ." (1961:71). From Genesis to Revelation, the Bible represents symbolically the human movement from nothingness to wholeness and experience of the totality of the psyche. Genesis begins with God's ordering of the outward world and continues with the creation of humanity, giving birth to the inner world. The drama of development begins when Adam is placed in the garden. The garden is not truly a paradise—that association is part of later projection onto the story, arising in the intertestamental period. It is not a human paradise; it is a state of childish unconsciousness. Therefore, Genesis does not describe the loss of paradise but the growth of awareness away from infancy.

In prohibiting eating the fruit of the tree, God speaks for the first time since chapter 1. Where the voice of God had been engaged in ordering the outer world, it now sets out to order the inner world. By setting limits that can be, and later are, transgressed, God performs another act of differentiation, offering Adam a choice.

Adam takes the first step out of unconsciousness by joining with God's creative work in naming the animals. The creation of Eve marks his encounter with the "truly other." The original androgynous unity of male and female must give way to differentiation if the man and woman are to be able to relate to each other. Westman states, "This would seem to imply that the psyche is whole in the beginning, suffers division and then must struggle to regain its original perfection" (285). The creation of Eve manifests the separation of the inner masculine and feminine, a separation that is as yet incomplete. They are still of "one flesh," and do not encounter one another as truly other until they eat the fruit and their "eyes are opened." Only then do they recognize their nakedness and otherness.

Westman contends that the story is not about the fall but about the very possibility of creativity both inwardly and outwardly. The breaking of the law marks an entry into true humanity. The inner world, like the outer, is engaged in the interplay of opposites and the necessity of differentiation and discrimination. Naming is not enough; that which is named must be weighed and valued. Still, one experiences movement toward growth as a "curse"—new awareness leads to new anxiety, as a widened perspective compels the psyche to relinquish its identification with the past. Curse and blessing express God's creative voice: "curse, because it is aimed at the psyche's primordial inertia; blessing, because as we hear it infancy ends and we are stirred to meaningful action" (83). He identifies original sin with the necessity to overcome the natural resistance to change and new ideas.

As awareness grows, a new symbol comes to the fore of the story—the tree of life. A simple "reaching out his hand" cannot find the way to the tree, a return to primordial unconsciousness; the flaming sword bars the way. Rather, it lies through the realities of human life, as Adam is set "*to cultivate* not only the soil, but *the very substance of his mind*" (84). It is only after the expulsion that the garden begins to emerge as a paradise. From the new perspective outside the garden, it appears not so much as a symbol of a lost innocence as one of potential wholeness. The river that flows out of Eden reaches the whole earth. This symbol of wholeness provides the backdrop for the unfolding of the biblical drama, but for now it recedes into the background as the dualities of human experience come forward in the conflict of Cain and Abel.

Motifs and Symbols

Others have commented on individual elements in the text rather than the whole. Jolanda Jacobi, a student of Jung's, uses the Genesis 3 story to illustrate some aspects of the process of individuation (1967). Consciousness comes into the primordial unity of the paradisial garden, characterized by unconsciousness, spacelessness, and timelessness. The eating of the forbidden fruit brings consciousness, which is first experienced as the breaking of a taboo, a "Promethean guilt" at overstepping human bounds. This consciousness of separation and difference—difference from God and the awareness of inner division, the opposites within the soul—forms the root of original sin.

Expelled from paradise, human beings now must take up the task of working back to the original unity in a new way. Individuation is precisely the process of working through the relationship of one's individual ego and one's unconscious depths, which still touch God. Individuation seeks to reunite what the genesis of consciousness divided. The act committed by Adam and Eve "became the source of all spiritual growth and drives us forward on the way to an ever higher development of the psyche and our world, to a consciousness of our relation to God and his workings in the soul through the symbols of the Self."

Rivkah Schärf Kluger, also a student of Jung's, examines the figure of Satan in the Hebrew Scriptures. She suggests that the serpent embodies the "dark side of God," enticing humanity to desire godlikeness. Identifying the serpent with Satan is strictly incorrect (though later tradition did so intuitively and most emphatically), yet it is still possible to speak of an affinity between their roles. The serpent, Satan, and the "sons of God" of Gen 6:1-4 all have a common purpose: to change the relationship between humanity and God. Unlike the more differentiated figure of Satan in the book of Job, who acts in concert with God, the serpent functions "behind God's back." So ambivalent and unconscious is the God of Genesis that, though human moral choice is what God really intends, he punishes the serpent and casts Adam and Eve from the garden. The serpent, then, symbolizes God's own shadow (Kluger 1967).

Francis Landy, in his study of the Song of Songs, also mentions this psychological tone of the serpent. He observes that the serpent embodies the ambivalence of Genesis 2–3. The serpent carries what is secret and unknown in the psyche, manifests the tension between opposites, and most particularly, "man's most intolerable wish, to destroy what is human, the trappings of culture, the reasoning, differentiating intellect" (1983:196).

Jo Milgrom: Amplification and Active Imagination. As we mentioned earlier, the techniques of amplification and active imagination, while producing fruitful engagements with the biblical text, are difficult to harness for critical work. Jo Milgrom's unique approach to Genesis 2–3 in her book *Handmade Midrash* provides an example of using amplification and active imagination to wrestle with the biblical text in a group setting. She describes a workshop in which she first leads participants in a close reading of the text, followed by psychological reflections taken from Edward Edinger's *Ego and Archetype*. She turns then to two works of art depicting the Genesis 3 tale: Michelangelo's *Temptation and Fall* and Chagall's *Homage à Apollinaire*. In exploring these works, she draws on additional material from Greek myth, the kabbalah, and midrash. Next, she invites the members of the group to experience the separation and grief implicit in the story by tearing strips of cloth and calling out words or sounds to express what is being felt and noting a word or fragment to be expanded by later writing. Finally, each participant uses the torn cloth to make a new construction and writes about the experience (1992). Milgrom offers examples of her students' art and writing as they emerged from the study. Their comments are intriguing for the personal issues that emerged for the students, but only one of the eight directly addresses the overall meaning of Genesis 3. This student, Caroline, was a participant in a different group who had used clay, rather than cloth, for the artwork. She observes how her work, a series of clay plates, manifested images that she later recognized while reading Edinger. It was on the basis of such spontaneously generated symbols, which appeared in the dreams, drawings, and fantasies of his clients, that Jung formulated his theory of archetypes. "My plate series," she writes, "can be seen as a development from total unconscious unity with God and my surroundings to a conscious awareness of my relationship with God" (86).

First, she notes, she used a circular form, representing herself. This circle she identifies with the inflated, godlike ego. Between the third and fourth plates she became aware of what was "surrounding and squeezing" her, and her fourth plate reflects the state of alienation described by Edinger. The last three depend on the fourth, as she reintegrates the shattered elements, moving in the individuation process to encounter God or the Self in a conscious relationship. She describes how the plates depict her own shifting center. The fourth plate differentiates "sacred" from "profane" space, upsetting the equilibrium of the first three. In the fifth plate, she brings a new order into what had been broken, incorporating the new dimension of the "sacred."

Caroline describes her plates as a "midrash on the biblical Fall," in which the snake is catalyst for Adam and Eve's discovery of consciousness. They also play a role as those who choose knowledge. They enter the world of time, space, and awareness. Their initial alienation is followed by self-forgiveness, beginning a lifelong cycle of development. Caroline chooses shapes that express movement and growth to symbolize this reality. She notes that the process of creating the plates itself entailed the experience of pain and suffering that lead to creativity and birth.

Milgrom observes in conclusion that what Caroline brought forth in her plates was, in fact, a tree. This projection of her self-image is akin to that tree in the garden. Only when Caroline chooses to discover what her life is about, to become conscious, does she develop a relationship with the tree of the story. Both the tree in Eden and Caroline's tree have their roots in the archetypal reality that transcends both.

It is significant that Caroline is the only student who does not use Milgrom's chosen artform with which to work. All the other students' reflections deal with grief and separation issues, which clearly the "ripping" and "calling out" medium of the exercise have evoked. While separation and grieving are part of the Genesis 3 story, the personal associations overwhelm the text itself. This fact shows that, while using active imagination in a workshop setting can be quite productive, translating it into critical form is very difficult. The students' engagement with the text is quite personal, their appropriation of the text significant. Yet communicating that process to others presents real difficulties.

COMPARISON AND COMMENT

Unlike the Freudian readings in the previous chapter, Jungian interpretations demonstrate remarkable consensus. All agree that the story concerns the dawning of human consciousness and that it shifts from symbols of completion, wholeness, or lack of differentiation (the mandala-like garden, the androgynous Adam) to images of separation, fragmentation, and alienation (guilt, nakedness, curses, suffering, and expulsion). The fruit of the tree of the knowledge of good and evil symbolizes consciousness and awareness of the opposites that constitute the whole of life.

Several factors contribute to this overall unanimity. Jungians are not as suspicious of the existing form of the text as Freudians and so do not attempt to recover some theoretical "original text." Interpretation of symbols by means of amplification is more flexible and inclusive than Freudian deciphering. Finally, Jungian interpretation works at a more generalized and abstracted level of discourse.

Text

Jungians most often deal with the text as it stands, rather than attempting to recover or reconstruct some proposed "text behind the text." This means that they are interpreting the "same" text and thus find greater convergence in interpretation. As Mario Jacoby observes, even when one takes into account modern biblical criticism of the text, the story as it stands makes consistent psychological sense and can be considered a legitimate elaboration of mythological statement.

Although Jungians assert that the text, myth, and manifestations of the unconscious are related, they understand that relationship differently than Freudians do. Freudians collapsed the distance between past and present and individual and collective. Jungian analysis, however, does not collapse the distinctions so much as bridge it by acknowledging that the (unknown) historical author, tellers of other mythic tales, and the contemporary reader all have the human psyche in common. Analogies between individual dreams and experiences, myths of differing times and cultures, and clinical experience are meaningful not because all these are precisely identical but because they share common grounding in human life. Jungians are thus free both to see what is common and to allow for what is different in the materials they study. They can draw upon historical and literary material, as well as psychological, to amplify and expand the symbols and relationships of the text.

Interpretation of Symbols

Jung understood symbolic language far more positively than Freud. Symbolism is the means of unconscious *expression*, not *repression*. The unconscious wants to be known and brought into consciousness. Symbols thus are not fundamental distortions or concealments; they are revelations of unconscious content. For this reason, Jungians are less suspicious of symbolic imagery and far more willing to accept mythic stories in the form in which they appear.

Amplification is a flexible method of interpretation that allows for wider diversity and inclusion of alternative possibilities. Because the aim of amplification is to expand and enrich the range of possible meanings of a symbol, one can allow for different interpretations without having to settle on the "best" meaning.

Two elements of the Genesis text stand out as evoking varying (yet not necessarily contradictory) interpretations: the serpent and the trees. Although all of these treatments agree that the serpent functions as a catalyst, enabling the man and woman to come to consciousness, several possibilities are given for its precise identity. Jung describes it variously as representing an individual's anima or as a shadow figure, either personal or collective. Kluger identifies it with the "dark side of God"—the divine shadow—and Landy affirms both its personal and divine aspects. What remains constant is that it is a manifestation of the unconscious.

While the serpent's identification may prove flexible, its function remains the same: it provokes a shift in consciousness. It may personify the drive for development and individuation, through either a more individual ego inflation (Edinger) or a more fundamental, transpersonal drive (Sanford). It may embody an inherent ambivalence in the polarity of opposites (Jacoby). The serpent is created by God (Jung, Sanford), or may in fact be a manifestation of God (Kluger, Landy), and ultimately brings a kind of deliverance, as the Gnostics had intuitively known (Jung, Sanford, Edinger). Thus, the serpent presents both individual and collective aspects. We might expect this fluidity of interpretation since above all the serpent is taken as symbolic of deeply unconscious material—material that is both personal and collective. The very essence of the unconscious is that one does not know or see it clearly by conscious reflection. One catches only glimpses and hints as they are manifested in symbolic form. One can discern its effects but cannot observe it directly. Taken together, these interpretations may vary in precise detail, but they agree on the psychic dynamics symbolized by the serpent.

Contrast these interpretations of the serpent with those of Otto Rank that we considered in the previous chapter. Rank took the serpent as a static symbol and related it to serpent images in other myths and neurotic fantasies, suggesting three contradictory interpretations that centered on the foundational assumption that the serpent can only be a symbol of incestuous relationship. By contrast, Jung's treatment of the serpent is based on its dynamic role in the narrative. He sees it as the personification of the (mother) tree, the "voice" of the tree. It may be the guardian of the tree, the keeper of the wisdom stemming from the knowledge of good and evil. Psychologically, it may represent either the shadow, unknown and repressed parts of the psyche, or perhaps the anima, the contrasexual dimension of the person that serves as psychic guide to the unconscious. Finally, it carries aspects of the tempter or destroyer, serving as the catalyst for a process (consciousness) that will disrupt and destroy the world of innocence.

Although both find multiple meanings for the serpent, their approaches contrast sharply. Jung affirms and exemplifies the polyvalence of symbols. The serpent need not signify one thing; it may evoke many different aspects of psychic interaction. Rank's "hard" symbolism requires that the symbol represent incest, but he cannot seem to find a single aspect that will adequately explain it. Where Freudian symbol interpretation seems static, Jungians focus on the function, development, and interaction of symbolic elements. Their process of expansion and amplification unfolds in the context of the particular elements of the story and their dynamic relationships.

The symbol of the tree of life is similarly undefinable in Jungian studies. All take the tree of the knowledge of good and evil as representative of the ability to discern, essential to consciousness, but they disagree as to the specific function of the tree of life. Jung offers differing interpretations: it can be a mother symbol; it is also the alchemical "philosophical tree" (*arbor philosophicus*), a symbol of individuation. Sanford identifies it with the "cosmic tree," which marks the intersection of heaven and earth in several myths. These identifications ultimately prove unsatisfying. The tree is evidently an emblem of life and immortality, but why should it be denied to Adam and Eve after their coming to consciousness? Jacoby suggests it is because consciousness is always time-bound and constrained by oppositions. The timeless world of the eternal tree and the temporal world of consciousness cannot coexist. Edinger and Westman both argue that although the tree of life represents the ultimate goal of psychic growth, it cannot simply be had for the taking. A flaming sword guards the way back to the tree of life; humanity can only move forward through the pain and suffering of the world. Edinger uses the Jewish legend that the tree of life is hedged around by the tree of knowledge to assert that only widening consciousness is sufficient to gain life.

Interpretive Framework

Jungian interpretations share a more generalized and abstract level of discourse. The overall framework of "coming to consciousness" is broader and more generic than the framework of the Oedipus complex. Within such a broad scheme, variations of detail are far less evident. None of these interpreters considers sexuality or incest to be a central theme of the story. The creation of Eve is important for its portrayal of the emergence of the male-female polarity out of androgynous unity, not as a comment on familial psychodynamics. Consciousness brings with it an awareness of opposites; awareness of sexuality is a *consequence* of Adam and Eve's action, not its cause or the act itself.

This shift in focus means that Jungians read Genesis against a different set of "parallel" world myths than those used by Freudians. They turn not to creation myths that use incestuous or sexual imagery to express human origins but to myths that emphasize stealing something from the gods. Thus, Prometheus and gnostic explanations of Genesis are considered parallels, not Oedipus, Canaanite theology, or South Pacific tales. At first glance the choice of material summoned by Jungians as "parallel" appears just as arbitrary as the oedipal canon of the Freudians. Yet there are significant differences both in the range of material and the nature of the associations to the Genesis text. While contending that orthodox and popular interpretations of the story are incorrect, Jungian interpreters nonetheless take the tradition seriously and attempt to explain why such interpretations arise and persist. "Sin and fall" are not the keys to the story's meaning, but human beings experience certain aspects of coming to consciousness as guilt, separation, and "original sin." Such language expresses significant dimensions of human experience, but as Sanford proves, the traditional framework of "sin and fall" leaves substantial issues in the text unaddressed. Freudians fail to account for traditional readings, other than to disregard them as missing the (unconscious) point.

In looking beyond traditional interpretations for other potential parallels, several writers turn both to heterodox gnostic tradition and to the Greek myth of Prometheus (Jung, Edinger, Sanford, and Milgrom). In considering gnostic understandings of Genesis 3, they emphasize the dynamics of coming to consciousness while disregarding gnostic dualistic cosmology, which considers the traditional God of the Hebrews a false god. Their use of the myth of Prometheus is quite different from the Freudian use of Oedipus and other myths. Prometheus has a narrative structure that parallels the events in Eden (theft of something belonging to the god[s]: fire and fruit) and painful punishment (physical restraint and torture: pain in childbirth and hard labor). Oedipus, on the other hand, is parallel only to the (interpolated and inverted) incestuous relationship between Adam and Eve. Other myths upon which Freudians draw are all associated at the level of details (serpent, tree, apples, etc.) and not through common narrative or function.

Criteria of Adequacy

On the whole, Jungian interpreters appear more successful at dealing with the entire text of Genesis 3 than Freudians. They are willing to deal with the narrative as it stands, and their interpretive framework, operating as it does at a higher level of generalization, leaves room for more of the story. That is, they concern themselves with broader movements and dynamics of the text rather than attempting a fragmentary analysis of each element in it. Without the Freudians' fundamental suspicion of mythic symbols, they are willing to accept the text as it stands and not seek concealed, disguised, or distorted "originals."

On the other hand, Jungian interpretations share with the Freudians an interest in universal patterns of symbolic expression more than the individual expressions themselves. While seeking to deal with the individual presentation of archetypal themes in this particular story, Jungian concern quickly runs to what is generic and universal, to highlight the collective and archetypal. For example, while the Jungians respect the framework of the story enough to maintain the woman (Eve) as a principal actor (as the Freudians did not, relegating her to an object in the oedipal dynamic), they are satisfied to identify her with the unconscious feminine and not to examine too closely the details of her conversation with the serpent.

Similarly, Jungian interpretation seems more successful at accounting for more elements in the text. The interpretive framework of "coming to consciousness" seems to fit the various elements of the story more completely than the oedipal dynamics favored by Freudians. Again, this might be due just as much to its more inclusive level of generalization as to the adequacy of the framework itself. Jungians, however, are not satisfied to seize on one element of the text and use it as the key to the whole. As Sanford remarks, any mythic or dream interpretation that fails to account for the whole text must be called into question. All the images—Adam, Eve, God, serpent, garden, and the trees—are included in a coherent whole. Not only are the various readings coherent within themselves, there is no jarring dissonance between them. Where there is disagreement, it is at the points of greatest specificity—the identity of the serpent, for example.

Jungian analysis is perhaps less successful at enabling the text to mean all that it can mean. Although Jungian psychology has a potential source for such enabling in the techniques of amplification and active imagination, for the most part these studies do not use them. At one level, Jungian amplification is no different from interpretive strategies common to any effort to understand a text, whether literary, historical-critical, linguistic, sociological, or political. Texts, models, or experiences that seem to deal with the same material as the text under consideration are mustered to illuminate desired aspects. The difference lies in the ultimate goal, and therefore they can treat the material as "parallel." While literary critics will draw on similar genres, and historical critics will look to contemporaneous writings, Jungian critics will cite other myths (collective) and dreams (individual) that seem to express similar archetypal phenomena.

Amplifying the Edenic images with images and symbolism from the ancient Near East would not only be possible, but forms the core of conventional biblical interpretation. Heinz Westman observes that the transformative power of symbols is found in the meaning "discernible only through amplification in relation to the context in which they are experienced" (1983:82). Yet this begs the question: *which* context of experience? For the present reader it is his or her own context that is primary. Yet does the original context in which the symbol arose have something to add to a reader's understanding? Our interpreters have not been slow to augment our current understanding with examples from Greek myth and gnostic exegesis. Why omit the more immediate setting of the Genesis text in the ancient Near East?

On another level, however, Jungian amplification is less workable as a textual strategy. In the therapeutic situation, the technique of amplification helps the analyst and analysand to distinguish more personal associations and meanings from those that are collective and archetypal. Acknowledging and expressing these personal connections to the text are difficult, at best, within the forms of currently accepted academic biblical criticism. Some forms of reader-response criticism do come close to acknowledging and examining such personal engagement with the text. For example, David Clines's introduction to *What Does Eve Do to Help?* represents his effort to be conscious of his own context for reading (1990).

For one thing, amplifications in Jungian practice are not usually in the form of (written) texts. They include images, feelings, intuitions, and other unquantifiable or even unrepresentable material. While personal associations are highly significant in an individual's appropriation of a text, they can also be idiosyncratic and far-ranging, even chaotic. Without the context of an analyst-analysand relationship, methods for evoking, confirming, and validating genuinely significant associations become problematic. As reader-response criticism becomes more generally accepted within biblical studies, however, attention to the process of amplification (through such means as comparative study of the interpretation history of a given text) may indeed yield fruit.

Jungian reading is not greatly concerned with the history or development of the text but is content to deal with the text in the form in which we receive it. In its effort to get at transpersonal and transhistoric archetypes, it can gloss over particularities of time, culture, and context. While the interpretive framework of "coming to consciousness" fits the story well, Jungian exegetes are content to accept that framework as the primary, if not the only, possible interpretation. Doing so leaves some important questions unaddressed. If, indeed, coming to consciousness is the core meaning of the text, why has the history of interpretation so often focused on sexuality? Why has theology claimed that the sin of Eden not only *feels* like sin but, in fact, is the *source* and *essence* of sin?

Finally, Jungian analysis can enable a reader's appropriation of the story. By asserting continuity between ancient and contemporary consciousness, Jungian amplification of mythic texts serves to bridge the distance between the present reader and the distant past and provides for identification and engagement with the story. One may not be able to relate to a forbidden tree, but one can well understand the dynamics of awareness, choice, and growth. Implicit in the assertion that the Eden narrative is an archetypal story is the implication that it unfolds an experience of the reader, as well. The reader is encouraged not only to study the text in the Bible but also to examine the "text" in oneself, to see how the two meet each other.

Jung's theories are not especially popular among theoretical psychologists today. They do find a place in clinical work. Many therapists believe that Jung offers a useful framework for finding meaning in an individual's life. In theological circles, Jung enjoys far greater esteem in the field of spirituality, with its concern for human transformation, than in conventional biblical studies, which have until recently been more analytical. Although Jungian approaches serve to explain psychological dynamics represented in the text, it is at the other end of Ricoeur's hermeneutical arc—appropriation—that they truly come into their own. The techniques of amplification and active imagination unfold the present meaning of the text and its impact upon the reader more than illuminating the original context. Amplification moves specific symbols from their context in the text into the realm of the general and universal, allowing the reader then to appropriate them in terms of his or her own particular life and experience.

How does this appropriation manifest itself? Note that Jo Milgrom's "handmade midrash" technique, while aiming specifically to enable participants to engage the story, does not result in the kind of appropriation expected in mainstream biblical criticism. Their responses are deeply emotional and highly idiosyncratic—appearing even banal—and are rooted in the particular experience and personality of each individual. Appropriation moves from the particular elements of the biblical story to the interpretive generalization of "coming to consciousness" and returns to particularity in the elements of the individual's own life. This is a form of active imagination, in which an individual becomes a part of the ongoing life of the symbol. While this engagement is highly significant for the individual reader's fuller appropriation of the text—both consciously and unconsciously—it is not easily harnessed to formal biblical criticism.

When measured against the criteria for psychoanalytic adequacy, these readings present us with an interesting paradox. They seem to meet the criteria quite well: they are fully coherent with Jung's theory and follow Jung's model of the psyche and its development. Indeed, for the most part, they are rooted in observations that Jung himself made about the text. They offer a way for the reader to read the story "therapeutically"—that is, not only as a dramatization of how human beings became conscious but as a guide for understanding one's own struggles to grow more conscious. Jungian interpretation thus encourages reading in a way that encourages personal growth and transformation.

Still, one wonders whether the theoretical framework of Jungian psychology is, in fact, necessary for making such an interpretation of the text. If one were to remove the technical vocabulary of "archetype," "anima/animus," "shadow," and "individuation" from these exegeses, what remained might still be a credible and intelligible interpretation from the perspective of a common human experience of growth. To what extent is it necessary to accept the Jungian model of the psyche in order to accept Jungian interpretation of Genesis 3 as valid?

6
A Myth of Human Maturation: Developmental Readings

Although there seems to be endless interpretation of the Gen 2:4b—3:24 myth, most readings are variations of the "sin and fall" theme. But this theme can be psychologically dangerous. It can prevent people from seeing and coping with actual reality and, instead, lead to a childish fantasy. . . . Fundamentally, the metaphysical guilt, the separation from reality, and the ego ideal of a perfect world and human nature prevent people from accepting and coping with actual reality and places people under the tyranny of an ego ideal. . . . the "sin and fall" type interpretation of life has the potential of retarding adult maturation and psychological well being.

—Bechtel 1994b

Within the many interpretations of Genesis 3, even the most nonpsychological of scholars have pointed out a developmental or maturational theme in the text. Joel Rosenberg describes from a literary perspective how the narrative segments of the story, while perhaps having their origin in diverse traditions, here consistently develop a theme of the development of human identity. He is concerned with issues of generational continuity, rather than individual personality, but nonetheless proposes that the story is "modeled on the human life-cycle" (1981:18). Although her primary concern is with historical theology, Anne Gardner states that, as is the case with all mythology, one can understand the story on many levels. One possibility is to read the story as a paradigm of human development from child to adult (1990).

Umberto Cassuto, who is hardly a psychological exegete, nonetheless finds the key to understanding the "parable" of Genesis 3 to be through human growth. Seeking textual parallels to the "tree of the knowledge of good and evil," he discovers that these words appear most often concerning the growth of small children. Humanity, he asserts, "was simple as a new-born child," and God's prohibition of the tree arises from "fatherly love." In disobeying the command, Adam is "like a child that disobeys his father. . . . He did not wish to remain in the position of a child who is under the supervision of his father and is constantly dependent on him; he wanted to learn by himself of the world around him; he aspired to become in *knowledge*, too, like God . . ." (1961:112ff.). In much the same way, both Samuel Driver and Hermann Gunkel comment that the transition undergone by the man and the woman in the garden is in some sense analogous to growth from childhood into adulthood. However, both picture this transformation in the garden as instantaneous, in contrast to normal development that takes many years (Driver 1904:46; Gunkel 1966:14–15).

Semanticist Ellen van Wolde is not at all surprised to find this "rather psychological orientation" in exegeses by such scholars as Cassuto, Gunkel, and Driver. In fact, she argues, a developmental theme is woven into the very core of the Gen 2:4b—3:24 narrative. Only once in the text, in 2:24, does the narrator speak directly. What seems a non sequitur, breaking into the story with a seemingly unrelated conclusion, is in fact an "iconic representation" of the entire sequence. Three components of the narrator's personal view are found in 2:24: first, "father and mother," second, "leaving," and third, "cling[ing] to his wife" and "becom[ing] one flesh." Genesis 2–3 is an expanded telling of this human development from dependent child through "necessary disobedience" and separation into mature independence and (pro)creativity (Wolde 1989:216–19).

While developmental interpretations of the paradise narrative from other perspectives have a psychological flavor, they remain general and metaphorical. Can one say more about the figures here than "they grow up"? Does a theory of the stages or issues of human psychosocial development add anything to the interpretation of the passage? Psychologist Erich Fromm and biblical critic Lynn Bechtel have each attempted, in quite different ways, to read the text in the light of developmental theory.

Erich Fromm: You Shall Be as Gods

Although trained as a traditional psychoanalyst in the Freudian mode, Erich Fromm was born into a family of Orthodox rabbis and developed an early love for the Bible's prophetic tradition and humanistic values. Fromm's humanistic psychology complemented Freud's concern for individual psychology with existential philosophy and an attention to social interactions influenced by Marx. Religion, he wrote, is "any system of thought and action shared by a group which gives the individual a frame of orientation and an object of devotion" (1950:21). He was concerned to differentiate between authoritarian and humanistic religion. "The question is not *religion or not*," Fromm declared, "but *which kind of religion*, whether it is one furthering man's development, the unfolding of his specifically human powers, or one paralyzing them"(26). Authoritarian religion involves submission to a power outside humanity; humanitarian religion, on the other hand, centers on human strength and capability.

In his exploration of the Bible entitled *You Shall Be as Gods*, Fromm describes the Old Testament as a document that traces the evolution of Judaism from an authoritarian religion "whose spiritual leaders insisted on the existence of one God and on the nonexistence of idols" to a humanistic "religion with faith in a nameless God, in the final unification of all men, in the complete freedom of each individual" (1966:9). The paradise story illustrates the vital first step in this evolution toward freedom. Adam and Eve's act is one of disobedience, yet the text never names it as sinful. It is rather the first act of freedom—the freedom to disobey, to say no. The traditional (that is to say, Christian) framework of "sin and fall" obscures the fact that the first human act is one of rebellion. Fromm declares that the story does not portray some fundamental change in human nature; it is rooted in historical experience, not metaphysical speculation. He does not mean to say that the story is a historical account but rather that it is a story that comes from actual human experience of rebellion and freedom. However, he does appear to consider it an evolutionary step in the historical past and not a universal human experience.

Psychosocial development of human beings is intertwined with an ongoing evolution of the conception of God. At the beginning of Genesis one finds the most archaic God image—that of an absolute ruler whose power is challenged by human freedom. Created in the image of God, the human creature seems ready to fulfill the serpent's promise, "you shall be as gods."

Fromm considers the idea that humanity could become God, and God's nearly frantic efforts to prevent it, to be an archaic part of the text. Why has it survived the process of transmission and redaction? Because, Fromm declares, it expresses a vital understanding of the essence of human nature—that human beings can be *like* God, a potential based in the idea of being made in God's image. While speaking of God, Fromm does not consider God to be an actual entity; at best, "God is a symbol of *man's own powers* which he tries to realize in his life, and is not a symbol of force and domination, having *power over man*" (1950:37).

The Bible clearly depicts the human capacity both for Godlikeness and for sinfulness. A capacity for evil seems just as inherent in humanity as the image of God. Sinfulness is not the result of a metaphysical "fall" but a necessary component of human freedom. The Bible presumes a genuine ability to choose between good and evil, which is the essence of free will. Humanity is, in a sense, an unfinished creation. Fromm quotes a Hasidic story that explains why the creation of humanity is the only act that God does not view as "good." It is because, of all God's creation, humanity is unfinished; human beings are "an open system, meant to grow and develop" (180). To live is to develop, and human disobedience is a necessary first step toward freedom to do just that.

The archaic, authoritarian God of Genesis, however, does not value freedom but obedience. He punishes Adam and Eve out of the need to preserve his supreme power by an act of force. (Given the patriarchal flavor of this archaic God concept, it seems appropriate to use the masculine pronoun.) Adam and Eve must submit in the face of overwhelming power, but they must never express any regret or repentance. This God acts according to the basic principles of authoritarian religion, a perspective in which the main virtue is obedience and disobedience the cardinal sin (Fromm 1950). Only later in the Bible text does the God image evolve beyond this authoritarian stage. The absolute ruler found in the first chapters of Genesis is transformed by the post-flood covenant with Noah into a "constitutional monarch," bound equally by the terms of the covenant. The third and final stage emerges with God's self-revelation to Moses as the *nameless* God of history.

Expulsion from paradise (which symbolizes the mother's womb) has a two-sided character since it is the beginning both of human history and of human alienation. Even as Abram's departure from home will later begin

Hebrew history, Adam and Eve's expulsion sends them forth into the world of self-awareness, choice, and independence. It is not a fall but an awakening. Yet this brave new world comes at the price of alienation and the loss of harmony with others and nature. Human beings must evolve beyond incestuous ties to "blood and soil" (as Gen 2:24 prefigures) (Fromm 1966:71). Fromm here uses the term "incestuous" in a metaphorical rather than literal sense to refer to the emotional ties to mother and father. This evolution from dependence to autonomy shatters preindividualist unity and brings conflict and struggle. Humanity is thrown into the existential tension of being simultaneously a part of nature and yet transcending it by self-awareness and choice.

Humanity still mourns the loss of oneness; ongoing desire to return to the primal union still shapes much of human life. Once human beings gain self-awareness and imagination, the "evil drive," the potential for sin, regression, and losing one's self becomes real. So it is that human beings will often wish "to give up reason, self-awareness, choice, responsibility and to return to the womb, to Mother Earth" (87). It is this desire that makes authoritarian religion so attractive.

There is truly no way to return. The cherubim guard the way to the garden; disobedience, self-awareness, and moral knowledge are irreversible. Humanity can only make its way by moving forward, by exercising choice and freedom.

Lynn Bechtel: Rethinking "Sin and Fall"

Unlike many of the other commentators we have read, Lynn Bechtel begins within biblical criticism rather than psychology. Several times she has argued meticulously for a "new interpretation" of Gen 2:4b—3:24, one that would avoid the shortcomings of the traditional "sin and fall" model. She uses a variety of methods to examine the text: literary, structuralist, sociological, and psychological (1993, 1994a, 1994b, 1995). The "sin and fall" model has many shortcomings: besides offering a negative view of human life and potential, and being a "misogynist's playground," this approach has no support elsewhere in the Hebrew Bible and apparently emerges only after the third century B.C.E. Modern exegesis using this model has declared portions of the text to be "irrelevant" or "extraneous," glossed over contradictions and illogical assertions, ignored dimensions of its symbols and wordplays that do not fit the scheme, and followed a historical approach that pays insufficient attention to its distinctive mythological features (1993:78–83).

Beyond its critical limitations, the "sin and fall" model is potentially dangerous psychologically. By idealizing a "perfect" world from which humanity has "fallen," it can encourage infantile fantasy thinking rather than genuine engagement with the ambiguity and tensions of life as it is. Further, it can engender feelings of unfounded guilt, hostility to the "fallen" world, and an unrealistic ego ideal that hampers mature living (1994b).

Bechtel offers an alternative interpretation—that the Eden myth is about the process of growth from childhood through adolescence into adulthood. Although Driver, Cassuto, and Gunkel recognized this theme of maturation, they were still too rooted in an individually oriented perspective to escape the assumptions of "sin and fall." In agreement with van Wolde, Bechtel argues that maturation is not merely one theme but the key to understanding the passage.

By analyzing individual symbols and their interactions, wordplays, and the structure of the text as it now stands, Bechtel proposes an outline of its literary structure. Using common elements of the theories of psychological development proposed by Jung, Piaget, Erikson, Kohlberg, Kohut, and Gilligan, she further refines her scheme. While differing in detail, these theorists agree on certain basic steps in childhood development. The initial tasks of infancy center on sensory and motor development, exploration of the environment, and developing a sense of trust. In early childhood a child begins to develop language. Middle childhood involves changing relationships with others and growing competency. Identity formation, sexual maturation, and the beginnings of intimacy are the tasks of adolescence, preparing for the productivity and generativity of adulthood (1994b). Thus, Bechtel argues, one can divide the story in this way:

Nature Foreshadowing the Human Maturation Process (2:4b-6)
Creation and Infancy (2:7-9)
Transitional Foreshadowing of Maturation (2:10-15)
Early and Middle Childhood (2:16-23)
(Perimeters, Social Differentiation, and Language Acquisition, Acquiring Social Identity)
Transitional Foreshadowing of Maturation (2:24-25)
Adolescent Maturation (3:1-19)

(Rite of Passage, Responsibility, Discernment of the Reality of Family Life, Adult Female Life, and Adult Male Life)
Transition into Adulthood (3:20-24)

Significantly, while Bechtel draws on modern theories of psychological development, she avoids the trap of imposing modern, individualized psychology on a text that one must interpret according to the ancient, group-oriented perspective. Identity comes from identification with the group; individual needs may be filled, but always within the context of the needs of the group. Two significant issues must be kept in mind. First, group-oriented societies cope with death in the context of group survival; they highly value procreation, marriage, and family. Second, the major form of social control is shame, not guilt. Shame entails a fear of group rejection for failure to live up to group ideals; growing up in a group-oriented culture involves becoming socialized to feel shame.

Nature Foreshadowing the Human Maturation Process (2:4b-6). Eden's tale begins with several oppositions that will appear throughout: high (heavens) and low (earth), uncontrolled and controlled (water and plants), limitation and potential. Limited by infertility, the unwatered land has the potential for growth. Its movement from infertility to fertility parallels the coming movement of humanity from infertile/unproductive child to fertile/generative adult. These oppositions (especially of possibility and limitation) are part of the very structure of creation; they are not the result of some yet-to-be-realized fall.

Creation and Infancy (2:7-9). The creation of humanity introduces another central opposition: unity and separation. An act of separation brings humanity into being. Wordplay between the Hebrew words for "human being" ('*adam*) and "ground" ('*adamah*) emphasizes the relationship of human and land. This interplay of unity and separation is "one of the most important dynamics in the myth and the individuation process" (4).The human being is placed in Eden, the "pleasing place," located in the east, the place of beginnings (of day or of life). The garden is protected; the boundaries of inside and outside are clear. It is the world of childhood, in which the child can safely explore, developing motor skills, autonomy, and a sense of trust.

Trees are found in this garden: trees for sustenance, and two special trees. The tree of life is a common ancient Near Eastern symbol, as we have seen, representing growth, maturing, and, especially to group-centered cultures, the continuation of life through seed. No prohibition is connected to this tree; it represents "recurring childhood with no progression toward adulthood or death"; to eat now from this tree would merely confirm "a child's view of life, an immature knowledge of life, which lacks an awareness of oppositional forces" (6). Bechtel calls this tree the "tree of the immature knowledge of life."

The other tree, the "tree of knowing good and bad" represents discernment, the ability to deal with the oppositional forces of life: good and bad. It is prohibited only to children, for eating from it will begin the process of maturation and identity formation. One can justly name it the "tree of mature knowledge of life." The presence of the two trees in the sheltered garden points to two important aspects of mature consciousness: ambiguity and the awareness of death. The question "two trees or one?" that has occupied critics testifies to the ambiguity. God's warning to the newly created human being in 2:17, inverted in the woman's conversation with the serpent in chapter 3, clearly associates the tree with death.

Transitional Foreshadowing of Maturation (2:10-15). Eden, then, symbolizes the protected world of childhood, watched over by a parent (God), which allows the child to explore securely yet contains the potential for maturing. The rivers of Eden themselves symbolize the theme of unity and separation essential to growth. Beginning as a single river in the childhood garden, the river divides into four streams that encompass the whole (outside) world. The river(s), the tree of knowing, and (presumably) the serpent, all present in the garden from the beginning, foreshadow the growth that must occur to prepare humanity for adult life outside the garden.

Early and Middle Childhood (2:16-23). God's prohibition of the tree of knowing sets boundaries for the child's world, introducing yet another dynamic tension between potential and limitation. The human being is not yet ready for the next step. A necessary next step involves development of language and social relations, for which the animals prove, indeed, "helpers" (2:18). In much the same way in which a child grows by caring for a pet, the human child will discover individual identity in relationship to the animals, exercise the capacity for naming and categorizing, and learn to relate to the "other."

To move toward adulthood, however, the child must develop social relations with other human beings. God creates another human from the human being while the being is in a deep sleep (resembling death). Sexual differentiation marks the next step in maturing. The two are one ("bone of my bones and flesh of my flesh"), and yet different; this new "woman" ('is-shah) is taken from "man" ('ish). Again, the wordplay emphasizes the close relationship between the two, attempting "to account for the powerful physical and psychological draw between the sexes" (8).

Transitional Foreshadowing of Maturation (2:24-25). Verses 24 and 25 present a key transition in the narrative, looking forward to adulthood, marriage, and family. Separation and union are expressed here in the man's leaving his childhood family and joining with the woman to create a new family. The fact that it is the *man* who must leave emphasizes the psychological nature of the separation; in patriarchal cultures it is usually the woman who physically leaves her childhood home. At the end of chapter 2, the man and woman approach the end of childhood; they are "naked, and not ashamed." They are still children without self-awareness or sufficient socialization to feel shame.

Adolescent Maturation (3:1-19). The serpent acts as catalyst for the next stage of maturation. The snake became emblematic of evil in later interpretation, but in earlier times it carried many potential implications. Its phallic shape and ability to renew itself by shedding its skin make it a symbol of sexuality and life renewal. It is wild and uncontrolled yet beneficial to agriculture by eliminating rodents. It is both known and unknown, as it moves above and below the surface of the ground. Serpents can also be deadly and poisonous; knowing with what kind of snake one is dealing is critical. The serpent becomes, then, a symbol of mature adult potential for discernment, for "street wisdom" required for survival; it is "wiser" than all the other creatures. Thus, the snake of discernment is associated with the tree of discernment. The serpent is a "natural" animal; the process of growth that it will trigger is also natural.

The woman is the one who interacts with the snake, perhaps because physiologically, women mature earlier than men, or perhaps because both the snake and women are associated with life renewal and wisdom. Bechtel notes that the woman receives her adult name before leaving the garden (3:20); the man is not named until he leaves the garden and becomes a father (1995). The serpent invites her to eat, knowing the potential for adult awareness. From her childish point of view, she can see only the potential (3:6), not the limitation, which will be the "death" of childhood (not immediate physical death). Like an adolescent, she sees only the good.

In eating the fruit, the man and woman become (self-) conscious for the first time ("their eyes were opened" [3:7]). The world does not change, only their perspective. They begin to see the world as it truly is. Their shame at their nakedness evidences their new consciousness. Connections between the serpent, nakedness, and shame are emphasized by similar sounding Hebrew words: "wise" (*'arum*), "naked" (*'arumim*), and "cursed" or "shamed" (*'arur*). The serpent is "wise" to their childish perception but later is shamed; they feel shame at their nakedness. Shame is a positive and necessary value in group-oriented cultures; it is a primary means of social control. They are becoming mature members of the community. They are afraid, not of death, but of being naked; their shamed hiding (not the act of a child) alerts God that something has changed.

Their act of disobedience does not destroy their relationship to God; it is only now that they begin to engage in full conversation with God. Not yet fully mature, they prove unable to accept responsibility for what they have done and seek to blame each other and the serpent. They have only begun the process, and God takes the lead in the next step by orienting them to the realities of human life. What the "sin and fall" model calls "curses" or "punishments" Bechtel contends are simply descriptions of the tensions of potential and limitation inherent in real life. Previously sheltered from the oppositions of the outside world in the safety of the garden, the man and woman now must learn about conflict and ambiguity.

The immature child had seen the serpent, a symbol of mature human life, only as potential (wisdom). God's words now accentuate its limitation. It will crawl on its belly (a shameful position) and its relationships (mature relationships) will be marked with conflict. On the basis of the status change implicit in the serpent's new body position (a common shaming technique in ancient warfare), in contrast to its previous high status, Bechtel proposes that "shamed" is a better translation than "cursed" (1993:92).

Turning to the woman, God emphasizes her potential for procreation and its limitations. Her ability to give birth is vital to the survival of the group and highly esteemed. Such power must be carefully controlled; the man's control of her sexuality aims at serving the group. Likewise, God addresses the man at the point of his potential to support his family by cultivating the earth. The ground's ability to produce inedible plants and the labor required will limit him. Death will ultimately limit him as well. Death, however, is presented neutrally; it is simply part of the cycle of life. It is a return to the beginning, to the womb.

Transition into Adulthood (3:20–24). A final wordplay suggests the woman's transition into adulthood. Her name "Eve" (*chavvah*), the mother of all "living things" (*chayyah*), emphasizes her potential as "life producer," a role requiring sexual maturity. God then prepares them both by clothing them (a sign of civilization, and social and psychological maturation) and sends them out.

They have now become like their parent, "knowing good and evil," and must be prevented from regressing to childhood perceptions. The tree of life (tree of immature knowledge of life), once unrestricted to them as children, must now be prohibited. What was appropriate, even necessary, for children is no longer adequate for adults.

Far from being a story of "sin and fall," Bechtel concludes, the garden narrative portrays movement toward maturity through increasing differentiation. From the unitary unconsciousness of childhood, one moves through awareness of the "other" and language development, sexual differentiation, and communal differentiation. Each step represents greater consciousness, freedom, socialization, and identity formation.

COMPARISON AND COMMENT

Although Fromm and Bechtel approach the text with concern for human development, they do so from significantly different frameworks and with diverging purposes. While Bechtel focuses on the Genesis text as an illustration of several stages of human development, Fromm's overall perspective includes the whole of the Hebrew Scriptures (and beyond, for example, the Talmud, Maimonides, and even Jesus). Within that broad span, the Genesis text represents only a single stage of development. Fromm's primary concern is with the evolution of human consciousness; he calls upon the text to illustrate one aspect of that evolution. Bechtel, on the other hand, is committed to interpreting the text itself, especially in contrast to the traditional "sin and fall" model.

The two developmental studies thus display contrasting attitudes to the text. Fromm reads the Bible as a record of the evolution of Judaism. The events of the garden, while not strictly historical, are a record of a historical experience. Fromm does not attempt an exhaustive exegesis—his intent is to trace the tensions between authoritarian and humanistic religion. He singles out one aspect of the story—human disobedience and God's punishment of it—and ignores details that do not fit. His theory is predominant; he subordinates the text to theory.

Bechtel, on the other hand, sees the text as having multiple dimensions. While she can illuminate some aspects psychologically, others require different tools. In making her case, she is careful to address every aspect of the text, linguistically, symbolically, literarily, and psychologically. For Bechtel, the text (and the framework for interpreting it) is primary; psychological theory is secondary. She frames her task in terms that recall Ricoeur's own criteria. A "new" interpretation of the text must be "an interpretation that would acknowledge the integrity of the text, incorporate all the existing symbols and synchronic themes, give meaning to the elements of the myth that have no meaning in the 'sin and fall' interpretation, and undergird the cultural assumptions and concerns of monarchical society" (Bechtel 1993:83).

Within such a comprehensive project, psychology becomes one tool among many, with its distinctive, but not exhaustive, contribution to make to the whole. Of her several articles, only one is explicitly "psychological," although psychological theories of development clearly lie behind all her work on the passage. In truth, Bechtel's explicit references to developmental psychology are quite general. While invoking the names of developmental theorists Piaget, Erikson, Kohlberg, Kohut, and Gilligan, nowhere does she cite them in detail, or refer directly to their work. Her only explicit references are to Karen Horney's concept of the ego ideal and Jung's model of growth from childhood fantasy to engagement with reality. She does not attempt to sort through the conflicting details of each of these theories; instead, she works at a level of generalization that all might accept. Rather than imposing a specific system on the text, Bechtel subordinates theory to the text, to the extent of allowing the forms within the narrative itself to shape her synthesis.

Both Fromm and Bechtel are sparing in their use of parallels. Fromm draws on other biblical texts and Jewish tradition but always relates both Genesis 3 and other materials to his evolutionary theory. Bechtel parallels the literary structures of the narrative and the stages of psychosocial development. Focusing on the uniqueness of this tale, she does not invoke other narratives or myths.

Unlike the interpretations we have seen under the auspices of the Freudian and Jungian schools, Fromm's and Bechtel's represent "psychologically informed" readings of the text more than "psychological readings." Fromm especially does not view the text as an account of individual psychic development. He considers it instead as expressive of an ancient and historical step in human consciousness and the evolution of the God image. Once achieved, one need not repeat it, and, in fact, later evolutionary steps have superseded it.

While Bechtel does find a pattern of individual maturation in the narrative, she escapes the trap of "psychologizing" by balancing aspects of individual development with social and historical factors. She is well aware of the pitfall of viewing the Hebrew Bible "from a modern perspective, without taking the different cultural factors into account" (1993:111). Social relations in a group-oriented society provide a counterbalance to psychological interpretation arising out of a modern individual-oriented society. Most significantly, Bechtel's clarification of the dynamics of "shame" in group-oriented cultures, as opposed to "guilt" in individual-oriented societies, sheds an entirely different light on the overall meaning of the narrative.

Symbolism

Bechtel's interpretation of the symbols of the story displays her multilayered approach. She begins with the historical context of the text (within the Israelite monarchy) and reads the symbols in the context of a group-oriented, agricultural society. She examines not only the individual symbols but their interrelationship. Only then does she move to elaborating their significance for social and psychological development. She takes symbols not as referring to aspects of the psyche or individual but to bundles of relationships.

Fromm shows little interest in the story's symbols. He pays no attention to the symbolic significance of tree, river, or serpent and makes only a passing cursory allusion to the garden as a symbol of the womb. Nor does he attempt to explore relationships among the figures in the garden. His concern is with only two relationships: the conflict of authority and rebellion, and the "incestuous" ties to family and land that must be broken.

"Sin and Fall" Model

Although both Fromm and Bechtel agree that the traditional "sin and fall" model for interpreting Genesis 2–3 is misleading, Fromm's exegesis still owes much to that very model. He asserts that the act of disobedience entails no cosmic alteration in human nature or the world, but that the essence of the tale is still to be found in disobedience/rebellion and punishment by a jealous God. The "archaic God image" exhibited in the story is a god of crime and punishment.

Bechtel's careful articulation of her "new" interpretation not only suggests an alternative but explains the weaknesses of the traditional framework. She can account for more of the text as it stands and can draw those strands together into an intelligible whole. In addition, she addresses the psychological effect on the reader of the traditional understanding. As evidenced in the epigraph to this chapter, Bechtel contends that the traditional "sin and fall" model can inhibit the development of a mature outlook on life by idealizing the childish image of fantasy of life without contradiction or conflict. "As long as commentators perpetuate the idea that limitation, pain, and death are punishment imposed on all of creation for human sin (an extremely egocentric presumption), human beings will neither accept life as God created it nor accept the Creator" (1993:109). Such fantasy can lead to a sense of guilt unfounded in reality ("metaphysical guilt"), the tyrannical "ego ideal" of artificial perfection described by psychologist Karen Horney, and hostility toward a fallen world.

While Bechtel's case for a maturational reading rather than the "sin and fall" framework is convincing, there are two issues that her interpretation fails to address. One is the fact that the term used to express the expulsion from the garden seems to have violent and forceful overtones. Departure from the garden seems to be more than simply a case of a parent sending a child off into the world. Secondly, her analysis does not account for the persistence and power of the "sin and fall" understanding of the story. If it is so inadequate, why has it dominated exegesis ever since the third century B.C.E.?

CRITERIA OF ADEQUACY

Evaluating these interpretations by our standards of adequacy is more difficult than with Freudian and Jungian efforts. These two treatments demonstrate the great flexibility developmental theory offers for interpretation of the text. Both Bechtel and Fromm address the text as a whole; they differ in what they consider to be the whole text. Bechtel's microcosmic analysis centers on Gen 2:4b—3:24, while Fromm's macrocosmic view encompasses not only this text but the whole span of Jewish religious history. Depending on the level of analysis and which aspect of development is under consideration, development-oriented theory is able to provide a coherent framework for understanding.

Developmental theory makes no claims of exclusivity or completeness. It contends only that there are certain aspects of human development that are common to all. The general framework and direction for understanding human growth or evolution offered by developmental categories must still be filled out with reference to the particularities of individual experience. For this reason, it is appropriate to describe developmental readings as "psychologically informed," rather than strictly "psychological." There is no overarching system into which every aspect of a text must fit.

Thus, the relative adequacy of developmental exegeses, as measured in reference to the criteria, will depend greatly on how the individual interpreter has filled in the details of the overall outline. For example, Bechtel finds it possible to draw upon literary, historical, and social methods to expand and support her developmental perspective. Because Fromm's plan is broader and more sweeping, he is less interested in addressing every detail of this particular story but consistently draws on tradition and contemporary experience to illuminate his point. Many aspects of a text will not relate specifically to developmental issues, and one must use other tools to aid in understanding them. For example, symbols may express some aspects of development but may also require historical or literary methods for interpretation. Interpretations that are quite adequate in illustrating developmental dynamics may at the same time overlook many other factors in the text that do not directly relate to maturation.

Because developmental theory is based upon observation of stages of maturing common to all human beings, developmental interpretations do enable a reader's appropriation of the story. Each reader can recognize that, at some level, this story is his or her own story and may help in self-understanding.

Judged by Ricoeur's criteria for adequate psychological explanations, developmental approaches measure up well. Both Fromm and Bechtel offer coherent, if widely differing, applications of developmental theory. It is somewhat difficult to evaluate Bechtel's use of theory in that she generalizes from a number of perspectives. Nevertheless, her chosen synthesis does make maturational aspects of the text intelligible. As for the potential of a therapeutic reading of the text, an appreciation of what constitutes healthy maturation provides a basis for identifying destructive or damaging understandings. This fact supports Fromm's argument against "authoritarian religion" and support of "humanistic religion." Similarly, Bechtel is concerned about how the traditional "sin and fall" interpretation of Genesis 3 can hinder "adult maturation and psychological well being."

7
Conclusion

Now the serpent was more
crafty
shrewd
subtle
cunning
cautious
prudent
clever
than all the living-things of the field that the Lord *God had made.*

—Gen 3:1

Our survey has taken us on many paths through the garden. As the literature on Genesis 3 amply shows, multiple interpretations are not only characteristic of reading the text from a psychological standpoint but from others as well. The characters and action in the story of the garden are so indeterminate as to be nearly universal. Man, woman, serpent, garden, tree, and eating are common elements worldwide, and they invite commentary from a multitude of perspectives.

We have examined one small corner of psychological approaches to this intriguing text. In light of our standards for criticism, how adequate have these Freudian, Jungian, and developmental approaches been for interpreting our chosen text?

FREUDIAN INTERPRETATION

All the Freudian analyses are characterized by disdain for the existing form of the text and based on a fundamental inversion of the existing story. Despite the narrative, they assert, Eve was not taken from Adam, but was Adam's mother. Centering their attention on the sexual/familial relationship of Adam and Eve, they interpret the story exclusively in terms of oedipal dynamics.

Collapsing distinctions between individual and collective, and past and present, they deal with the story as though it were a dream or symptoms manifested by a client in therapy. Thus, their interpretations of symbols range through such divergent contexts as ancient Near Eastern stories and symbolism (for example, the tree of life in Adapa and Gilgamesh stories and serpent goddesses), world mythology (notably Oedipus, but also Nordic, Pacific Islands, and African myths), and contemporary dreams (dreams of serpents or eating as symbolic of incest and coitus).

Interpreting symbols statically rather than dynamically, these studies fragment and isolate individual figures from the story (tree, serpent, woman-mother) and identify them with mythic elements and dream images without regard for differences of context or function. Each element is important primarily for its usefulness in fitting the story into the framework of oedipal dynamics.

Given this fundamental disregard for the existing story, and an atomizing approach in which a few details are made to serve as the key to the story, it is no wonder that Freudian studies do not measure up well to standards of critical adequacy. Freudian interpreters do not deal with the whole text, choosing either to reconstruct a theoretical "original" text (Rank, Róheim, and Reik) or simply to focus on one or two aspects to the exclusion of others (for example, Fodor's and Jork's attention to Eve as mother-goddess). By telescoping distinctions of time and personality, they obliterate the uniqueness of the story, reading it as simply one of many oedipal myths.

Even within the limited range of their analyses, they do not always achieve coherence or convergence. Thus, for example, Rank speaks of Eve at various times as mother and wife to Adam, and as daughter and wife of God. In much the same way, he proposes conflicting meanings for the serpent—as a symbol for Adam, for an incestuous God, or for God as a father defending his daughter.

In general, the Freudian tendency to reductionism prevents these interpretations from unfolding all the potential meaning of the text. However, one genuine contribution of Freudian analysis is the recognition that more is at work in texts and symbols than conscious communication of meaning. In addition, their attention to sexual imagery in the story may help to explain why so many people have understood it to have something to do with sexuality.

Ultimately, Freudian interpretation is not likely to lead one to appropriation of the story. While one might come away from these interpretations impressed at the ingenuity of these authors at fitting Genesis 3 into an oedipal framework, one is not likely to appreciate the story itself or understand what relationship it might have to the reader.

JUNGIAN INTERPRETATION

Genesis 3 fares better at the hands of Jungian interpretation because the interpreters, without exception, take the present form of the story seriously. Jungian amplification offers a more flexible and inclusive approach to symbols. The interpretive framework of "coming to consciousness," which characterizes all of the studies, is more general and comprehensive than the oedipal structure. It is dynamic, rather than static, leading from images of completion and wholeness (the garden, the undifferentiated human) to representations of fragmentation and alienation (guilt, suffering, and expulsion). As we have noted, maturation is a key theme that is woven into the structure of the text itself and requires no inversion or distortion of the story.

Jungians read the text, myth, and dream imagery as similar, but not identical, manifestations of unconscious material. Thus, while identifying common themes and symbols, they still respect the individuality of each. They accept the Genesis story as it is presented in the canonical text and seek to understand each element in it.

Jungian interpretations respect the individuality of the text and, far more thorough and coherent than Freudian ones, stand up better to the criteria of adequacy. The framework of "coming to consciousness" not only addresses the text more fully than the Freudian oedipal scheme, but even more completely than the traditional "sin and fall" model. Weaknesses in the Jungian approach arise from the very generalizations that make coherent interpretation possible. In seeking out transpersonal and archetypal levels of meaning, Jungian interpreters at times gloss over certain particularities of the text. Most notably, they give peremptory effort to exploring the historical and cultural context of Genesis within the ancient Near East. Further, while the interpreters deal with traditional understandings of the text, they do not adequately explain why the text is so often read in sexual terms.

Because it is grounded in archetypal understanding, which by definition is universal to all human beings, Jungian exegesis offers an authentic point of engagement with the text for the modern reader. By asserting that the core of the story is about human experience that all share, these interpretations enable the reader to identify with the text and engage it in their own lives.

DEVELOPMENTAL INTERPRETATION

Developmentally based interpretations are more diverse than either Freudian or Jungian approaches. Because developmental theory claims only to deal with the dynamics of human maturation in broad outline, the form that individual applications take is greatly dependent on the writer's chosen framework and how he or she draws upon other interpretive methods to fill out that outline. Since many readers have noticed themes of maturation and growth in the Eden narrative, developmental perspectives offer quite appropriate models for amplifying those aspects. The strengths and weaknesses of developmental interpretation for interpreting the text are due less to the underlying theory than to how well or thoroughly a given critic uses additional critical tools.

Although Fromm and Bechtel share a concern for identifying social and maturational dimensions of the Genesis text, they differ greatly in their aims and methods. Fromm's macrocosmic view describes the events of Eden as a single stage in an evolution that spans the whole of the Hebrew Bible and subsequent Jewish tradition. Bechtel's microcosmic view analyzes Genesis 3 in detail, identifying a number of stages of early childhood development reflected in the text.

Fromm's wide-ranging perspective leads him to distill the story to a single aspect (disobedience and punishment), ignoring other details that do not fit his overall theme. His key point, that disobedience to authority is a necessary step in coming to maturity, is in accord with the growth theme in the narrative. His fragmentary analysis of Genesis 3 does not fulfill Ricoeur's standards well. He does not deal with the text as a whole, omits most of the elements, and remains coherent by virtue of his selectivity. His concern, however, is not this single text but the overall development of the images of God and humanity as religion evolves from an authoritarian system to a humanistic one.

Of all the studies we have considered, Bechtel's is by far the most comprehensive, expanding and supporting her psychological observations with a number of other critical tools. She is the one interpreter who demonstrates familiarity with a variety of methods for biblical study and is the most attentive to the text *as text*. She uses structuralist, literary, narrative, and linguistic methods to analyze various aspects of the text, fitting them into her chosen developmental pattern.

Bechtel's overall approach builds on the maturational theme inherent in the text. Her outline of the text's structure follows the narrative as it stands, accounting for each episode in sequence, marked by wordplays, key symbols (garden, trees, serpent), and themes (unity and separation, potential and limitation). Her analysis is not limited to literary structures; she is also careful to spell out the historical context of the story within a shame-based culture, in contrast to guilt-based modern Western cultures. Thus, when she fleshes out her outline with reference to developmental psychology, she avoids the trap of psychologizing—an anachronistic application of modern psychological theory to the ancient text. Bechtel gives full respect to the text and its historical context; theory is subordinate to the text.

For these reasons, Bechtel's treatment clearly meets the criteria most fully. She deals comprehensively with the whole text, offering an interpretive framework that fits nearly every aspect coherently. She carefully analyzes those aspects that make this text unique, both with reference to its structure and literary devices and to its historical and social context. Her use of developmental psychology provides a point of identification between the text and the reader, who can identify the story as his or her own story. Even more, she is concerned for the psychological damage that the traditional "sin and fall" understanding of Genesis 3 can do and seeks a more "therapeutic" understanding.

The weaknesses of Bechtel's approach paradoxically arise from the very factors that make it compelling. She is far less attentive to the details of the psychological theories she invokes than she is to the text. Because she subordinates theory to the text, she generalizes differing developmental psychologies to the point that details of each are lost. Further, in her effort to promote a maturational view of the text, she glosses over the violence of the expulsion and offers no explanation for why the "sin and fall" understanding has had such power through the centuries.

CONTRIBUTIONS

Each of the approaches has something unique to offer to the interpretation of Genesis 3. All describe dynamics and relationships in human development or the depths of the psyche that are common to all human beings. In addition, they offer clues as to why certain interpretations centering on sexuality, disobedience, guilt, and "fall," which may be poorly supported by the text persist nonetheless.

Even though it measures up poorly to the evaluative criteria, Freudian interpretation alerts us to the fact that language is not simply transparent, and that speakers and writers sometimes will have both conscious and unconscious reasons to modify what they say. A recognition that multiple factors work together in determining the meaning of a text will sometimes require a "hermeneutic of suspicion," based on an understanding of the psychological dynamics that may affect communication.

Also, the fact that the "knowledge" in the story is so often identified as sexual awareness or activity suggests that one must at least take Freudian interpretations seriously (Cunningham 1991:122). The incest theme may refer not so much to actual incest but to a dynamic of intimacy, separation, and competition to which the story points. Whether or not the symbols of the story are primarily sexual, they certainly must have sexual overtones. If, as the Jungians and Bechtel argue, the text is not fundamentally about sexual transgression, why has that idea turned up so often in the history of interpretation? It may be that the advocates of a maturational perspective have paid insufficient attention to the powerful role that sexuality plays in human growth. As a child comes to consciousness and matures into adulthood, he or she often experiences sexuality as compelling, troubling, and the source of much conflict, often with parents. Whether or not one accepts the Oedipus complex as an accurate and adequate explanation of the parent-child relationship, it is certain that issues of sexuality, intimacy, jealousy, freedom, and dependence are closely intertwined.

Both Bechtel and Jungians show convincingly that the traditional (at least since Augustine) understanding of "sin and fall" does not fit the details of the text adequately and raises more questions than it answers. Bechtel sees clearly the psychological damage that the traditional model can have on individuals, but she is not able to explain why such a damaging perspective should have such power. This is due in part to her careful distinction between guilt and shame. In its original context of a shame-based culture, the story is not about guilt. However, contemporary readers, embedded in a guilt-based culture, will tend to read guilt into the text. Guilt feelings form the basis of the "sin and fall" response. It remains for the Jungians to elucidate the unconscious dynamics of guilt and betrayal stirred up with the dawning of consciousness. Concepts such as ego inflation, the shadow, and the inherent conflicts of individuation enable Jungians to explain more fully how sin, guilt, and fall relate to Genesis 3. However natural and necessary growth and maturity may be, there is a corresponding natural (and even necessary) resistance to that process. Separation from union with the cosmos brings with it a sense of inadequacy, failure, and loss, which come to be expressed in terms of sin and fallenness. This new consciousness appears as something that the Other (God/parent) possessed before; it must have been "stolen" in some way. The benefit of expanded capability to know and live in the world is counterbalanced by the requirement that one relinquish cherished intimacy with the parent and the world. It seems a "Luciferian" act, a description that plays on the close association of the light bringer and the devil. "Original sin" is more than a theological category; it articulates the conflict between the need for individuated consciousness and a desire to return to the womb of blissful union.

WHICH INTERPRETATION IS MOST ADEQUATE?

Bechtel's study, as we have seen, best fulfills Ricoeurian criteria of adequacy overall. Her careful analysis of the text provides a solid basis for identifying and elaborating developmental themes and provides a model for careful reading before attempting psychological elaboration. Her multidisciplinary method and careful distinction between guilt-based cultures and shame-based cultures enable her to avoid anachronistic application of psychological theory. Hers is the most successful interpretation of the story within its historical context.

However, Bechtel's effort is less successful psychologically. She generalizes and homogenizes developmental theories to the point that, though none of her chosen theorists might object to her analysis, each of them would have more to say about the dynamics and details of each stage of development. The success of Bechtel's approach is due more to the fact that she is familiar with a variety of methods of biblical interpretation and can select the appropriate tools for getting at different aspects of the text than to the inherent superiority of the developmental perspective. Peter Homans has argued that developmental perspectives do provide a uniquely appropriate framework for hermeneutical efforts. He suggests that the "structuralist" (his term for developmental) theories of Piaget, Kohlberg, and Loevinger provide a helpful model for understanding the key issues of the interrelationship of subject and object, and the relationship between the two. Developmental orientation is helpful because it is cross-cultural, oriented to the development of relations to the other and otherness, and open enough to allow for integration of other psychological models (Homans 1975). Bechtel is not only able to summon multiple psychological models, she is ready to call upon literary and historical models as well. The text is not simply an expression of psychological phenomena and Bechtel's use of several approaches enables her to achieve a more comprehensive interpretation.

Psychologically speaking, John Sanford's treatment of the text is more adequate than Bechtel's. While he does not have the breadth of Bechtel's knowledge of tools for biblical criticism, nevertheless he does deal with the whole text in a coherent and consistent manner. His use of Jungian concepts is deeper and fuller than Bechtel's handling of developmental theory, and his conclusions about the text parallel hers to a great extent. There is little conflict between Jungian views and those of Bechtel. Bechtel, in fact, cites Jung as one of her sources, and Jungians have often turned to developmental theories in order to fill out gaps in Jung's work. Bechtel's observation that the literary structure of the text parallels stages of human maturing provides a more detailed support for Sanford's intuitions. A combination of the two perspectives might prove quite helpful. Bechtel's attention to literary and sociohistorical issues counterbalances the Jungian tendency toward overgeneralization, while Sanford's understanding of the psychodynamics of coming to consciousness serves to explain the origin and endurance of "sin and fall" overtones.

Bechtel's work is more likely than Sanford's to find a welcome in biblical studies as presently constituted. Besides employing literary, structural, and historical methods familiar to others in the field, she relies on a generalized social-psychological theory founded primarily on outwardly observable social behavior and socialization. In her formulation of psychological elements, she avoids specialized language or detailed exposition of developmental theory. Freudian and Jungian explorations of the text are complicated by references to the unconscious, as well as technical vocabularies and interpretive methods peculiar to their theories. If a reader remains unconvinced of the reality of the unconscious, depth-psychological methods of criticism will seem a waste of time.

SUGGESTIONS FOR FUTURE PSYCHOLOGICAL BIBLICAL CRITICISM

The strengths and weaknesses of this small selection of studies from Freudian, Jungian, and developmental perspectives suggest several factors that should govern psychological biblical criticism. These issues are not unique to psychological criticism; they are considerations that should govern any efforts at exegesis. However, as we have seen, they are factors that, for the most part, have been particularly problematic in psychological approaches.

First of all, one must recognize the *text as a text.* A text is different from an individual in the therapeutic situation. A text differs from face-to-face discourse in that the speaker is no longer present. The world in front of the text, projected by the polyvalent possibilities of language, replaces the immediate referential context in which a speaker can clarify and refine intended meaning through dialogue and correction. In the analytical situation, techniques like free association and amplification can be immensely valuable for uncovering and clarifying unconscious elements. In such a situation, further conversation and additional material from the client fulfill the function of validation and confirmation of interpretation. A fundamental problem with Freudian interpretations begins with their assumption of identity between the text, myths in general, and individual dreams. Although Levy, Fodor, Jork, and Reik all allude to the fact that the text has undergone editing by the tradition, they do not consider how this editing may make the text different from a dream. This initial assumption of continuity leads to confusion of method and abuse of the text.

Recognition of the text as text leads to a second concern. Bechtel's interpretation is successful in part because of her careful analysis of literary structures and their historical context. However mythic the roots of biblical stories may be, they have still gone through a long history of composition and redaction. Thus, the interpreter must take care to recognize literary conventions, genres, and context. One must be sure not to read metaphorical or literary formulations as though they were literal expression. Symbols are not simply eternal and unchanging; there is an interplay between persistent and universal symbols, and their interpretation and elaboration in different times and cultures. For example, Bechtel shows that if one fails to take into account the difference between shame-based and guilt-based cultures, one will miss how developing shame at one's nakedness can be a positive development.

Third, more successful interpretation will work at an appropriate level of generalization. Psychological theory is based on observation of the behavior of individuals and communities. Accuracy and reliability of theoretical constructions rest upon demonstrable concrete examples. Given the relative meagerness of biblical material and the lack of access to the individuals behind the text, most conclusions about psychological dynamics and phenomena in the Bible can only be based on a presumption that ancient and modern human psyches are in some sense parallel. Without a way to establish the extent of that parallelism, psychological exegesis cannot meaningfully deal with every minute detail in the text. Freudian exegesis remains largely unconvincing precisely because of its unsupported assumption that all myth, dreams, and neurotic phenomena are identical, and its tendency to make definitive pronouncements about the significance of tiny details. Bechtel, in sharp contrast, applies a more generalized and suggestive perspective. Sanford deals with the text by suggesting possible answers to the questions a reader might ask. Critics must exercise a certain humility, remaining somewhat general and tentative, and suggest possibilities rather than stating absolutes.

Finally, those attempting psychological criticism will benefit from the recognition that psychology is just one of the factors that affect meaning, and a willingness to draw upon other disciplines. Freud himself noted that psychic phenomena are overdetermined—that is, any given symbol or dream image may reflect many unconscious sources. Literary phenomena are similarly overdetermined; they are shaped not only by psychological components, but by many others as well—historical, political, economic, social, rhetorical, etc. Bechtel's analysis succeeds because it is multidisciplinary, using appropriate interpretive tools to uncover different levels of the text. Psychological methods are essential for getting at unique dimensions of a text but psychological criticism that is not carried out in conversation with other modes of exegesis runs the risk of becoming mere psychologizing.

CONCLUSION

Our tour of the garden has led us to encounters with the strengths and weaknesses of just a handful of psychologically informed biblical criticisms. We have seen how psychological criticism can make unique contributions to biblical studies, identifying and describing psychological dimensions of the structures, symbols, and relationships of the Genesis 3 account. Each of the three perspectives brings its characteristic methods of exegesis to bear on the text, each with its respective strengths and weaknesses.

Several questions remain about psychological criticism of Genesis 3. Why have popular interpretations of the text involving "sin and fall," sexuality, and guilt persisted despite being unsupported by the text? We have suggested some tentative preliminary answers to that question, but it merits further careful reflection. Is it possible to bridge the distance between scholarly analysis of the text and the ways modern readers actually read the story? Can psychological reflection help us to understand why this story continues to fascinate us? Jung and Freud both claimed acquaintance with and interest in the Bible; they and other psychologists are themselves embedded in Western culture. How were their own theories of sexuality (for example, the relationship of masculine and feminine), personality, and guilt shaped by the legacy of Genesis 3?

In a previous generation Rudolf Bultmann taught his students to be suspicious of psychology. That suspicion might have been well founded in his day, when modern psychology was still in its infancy, and critics applied it to the Bible as yet another historical tool. But Freud taught us long ago to be suspicious of consciousness, and Jung called us to recognize that Scripture is the utterance of the soul. Biblical scholars are coming to know that there is more to the text than the intellectual, the historical, and the conscious.

Glossary

absolute knowledge (Jung): The unconscious knowledge, not mediated through sense perceptions, of objective reality. It underlies precognition, telepathy, and instinctive behaviors.

active imagination (Jung): A process of reflecting imaginatively on a symbol, dream element or fantasy and allowing it to unfold further. Also called "dreaming the dream onward."

alchemy: The medieval philosophy of alchemy centered on the search for the process that would turn lead into gold. Jung considered alchemy a projection of the psyche's drive to transformation.

amplification (Jung): A process of identifying meaningful associations and feelings connected to a symbolic or dream element, similar to the Freudian free association.

analytic psychology: The psychological approach developed by C. G. Jung (1875-1961) and his followers.

anima: The Latin translation of the Greek "psyche," meaning "soul" or "life principle." Early church writers on the soul like Tertullian and Augustine used the term. In Jungian psychology, the anima is the archetype representing the feminine element in a man.

animus (Jung): The masculine principle in a woman, corresponding to a man's *anima*.

archetype (Jung): Characteristic ways of patterning psychic experience rooted in the collective unconscious. Archetypes themselves are unobservable directly but are expressed in symbols, myths and dream elements.

behaviorism: Psychological theory that focuses only on observable behavior as a response to stimulus.

cognition: The process of knowing or thinking, including awareness and discernment.

cognitive dissonance: The condition of recognizing disjunctions between one's expectations or worldview and one's lived experience.

collective unconscious (Jung): That part of the psyche that is universal and impersonal; all human beings are connected to the collective unconscious. It is inherited, not developed, and is the locus of the *archetypes*.

condensation (Freud): In dream images, the process by which several elements may be combined into a single object or representation.

conscious: That part of the human mind that is self-aware, rational and knowing. It is contrasted with the unconscious.

depth psychology: Those theories, most notably Freudian and Jungian, that deal with unconscious material.

developmental psychology: Psychological theories that focus on the process of individual mental and social development.

differentiation (Jung): The separation of a part from a whole to allow for its individual development.

displacement (Freud): In dream images, the process whereby an element replaces another.

ego: The center of conscious functioning in the psyche; self-awareness. In Freudian theory, it makes up the totality of personality along with the id, the source of psychic energy or libido, and the superego, the unconscious center of control. Jung understood the psyche as containing the ego, the personal unconscious and the archetypes of the collective unconscious.

Eros and *Thanatos* (Freud): Taken from the Greek words for love and death, they are the unconscious drives toward life and union (Eros) and toward death and disintegration (Thanatos).

false consciousness: An ideology or understanding founded on self-delusion, usually unconscious. Such delusion can be psychologically-, ideologically-, or socially-based.

family systems theory: Psychological theories that examine the family as a system of interacting relationships and dynamics and not simply as an aggregation of separate individuals.

Freudian psychology: The psychological system developed by Sigmund Freud (1856-1939) and his followers. It understands human personality to arise from the interaction of the *ego*, *id*, and superego. An individual's inability to function appropriately is rooted in childhood experiences (most notably the Oedipus complex) that have been repressed into the unconscious. The therapeutic technique of psychotherapy is aimed at identifying those traumatic elements and bringing them back into consciousness.

hermeneutic of suspicion (Ricoeur): The recognition that unconscious factors are always at work in the process of interpretation.

humanistic psychology: Psychological theories that emphasize the human capacity for self- understanding, self-healing and finding one's authentic identity.

individuation (Jung): The process of becoming fully an individual through conscious encounter with the archetypes.

inflation: In relation to the ego, an unwarranted sense of self-importance, omnipotence or invincibility.

inversion (Freud): In dream images, the process in which an element is changed into its opposite.

Jungian psychology: The psychological system developed by Carl Gustav Jung and his followers. It understands human personality to involve the relationship between the conscious mind and the archetypes that are shared by all human beings. The goal of human development is individuation, the process by which one integrates unconscious elements into the whole of the psyche. Jungian therapy is known as analytical psychology.

latent content (Freud): The unconscious material that underlies dream images, contrasted to the manifest content.

lateral specialization: The way each side of the brain controls different functions of *cognition* and behavior.

learned helplessness (behavioral psychology): A state of listlessness and inability to adapt to the environment observed in animals subjected to unpredictable stress.

literatherapy: A therapeutic technique that invites a client to identify with characters in a story or narrative in order to help them conceptualize their own situation and find solutions.

mandala: The Sanskrit word for "circle." In Eastern religions, mandalas are elaborate circular representations of the cosmos. Jung discovered that mandalas appeared in religious rites around the world and were spontaneously produced by his own patients. He believed that the mandala was both a representation of, and a tool to enable individuation.

manifest content (Freud): The surface meaning of a dream, myth or fantasy after the unconscious latent content has been concealed by processes of condensation, displacement, inversion, merging, or splitting.

merging (Freud): In dream images, the process in which two or more elements are joined together.

myth of the primal horde (Freud): A theory that in prehistoric times our pre-human ancestors lived in a band led by an alpha male who controlled access to the females. At some point, the young males banded together to kill and consume the leader, but were then overcome with feelings of remorse. Freud located the origins of religion in the rituals that were developed to commemorate and atone for that crime.

Nachleben: The ongoing effects of a biblical text; its impact on readers and communities across time, as opposed to the *Sitz-im-Leben* (setting in life), its original social setting.

narcissism: The quality of self-centered personality characterized by the need for attention and an inability to relate empathetically with others.

neurosis/ neurotic: Neurosis is a generic term used to describe any psychic disturbance or imbalance that is less severe than psychosis.

Object relations psychology: Psychological theories that focus on the relationships between an individual and various "objects." Objects can be external– people, places or things– or internal– memories, representations or fantasies.

Oedipus complex (Freud): The stage of psychological development in which a young boy develops (unconscious) sexual feelings for his mother and views his father as a rival for her affections.

overdetermination (Freud): The idea that any given unconscious element, such as a dream symbol or mythic motif, may represent many different psychic processes of representation and concealment.

personal unconscious: The portion of the unconscious specific to the individual. For Freud, the whole of the unconscious was personal; but Jung believed that every individual participated in the collective unconscious in addition to their personal unconscious.

plurivocal, polysemic, polyvalent (Ricoeur): The inherent quality of language to "speak with many voices," that is, to carry multiple meanings, and to do so at multiple levels of denotation and connotation.

projection: The mechanism by which an individual attributes to others qualities or factors that, in fact, reside in his or her own unconscious.

psyche: The Greek word for "soul" or "life principle." In contemporary usage it refers to the psychological totality of a person, including both conscious and unconscious dimensions.

psychoanalysis: The therapeutic application of Freudian psychology.

psychodynamic: Describing the interactions of psychological factors, especially at depth.

psychologism: Reducing a phenomenon to purely psychological categories.

psychology: The systematic, scientific study of behavior, whether directly or indirectly observable.

repression: The process by which something becomes unconscious, or the process of keeping something from emerging into consciousness.

Self (Jung): The central archetype of wholeness and completion related to the psychic God-image.

shadow (Jung): The archetype corresponding to the rejected, weak and underdeveloped in the psyche.

splitting (Freud): In dream images, the process in which an element is separated into two or more images.

stage theories: Developmental theories that describe consistent and predictable patterns of human psycho-social development.

symbol: A symbol is something that represents something else. Freud and Jung both believed that symbols were a means of connecting to the unconscious. Freud felt that the purpose of symbols in dreams and myths was to conceal unconscious meaning. In contrast, Jung considered symbols to be expressive of unconscious material that otherwise would be unknowable.

transitional object: In Object Relations theory, a transitional object is an object like a blanket or toy in which a child invests great love and care and that enables the child to learn how to establish relationships with other people.

unconscious: The unconscious is the part of the psyche that is unknown to the conscious, self- aware mind or ego. While Freud divided the psyche between the conscious and the unconscious, Jung further distinguished between the personal unconscious and the collective unconscious.

union of opposites (Jung): Essential to the ultimate totality of individuation, the union of opposites refers to the process of bringing opposing elements into balance with one another.

Bibliography

Citations from Jung's *Collected Works*, hereafter abbreviated as *CW*, refer to paragraph numbers, rather than page numbers.

Abel, E. T. 1971. "The Psychology of Memory and Rumor Transmission and their Bearing on Theories of Oral Transmission in Early Christianity." *Journal of Religion and Health* 51:270–81.

Aichele, G. et al.. 1995. *The Postmodern Bible*. New Haven: Yale Univ. Press.

Alter, R. 1981. *The Art of Biblical Narrative*. New York: Basic.

———. 1992. *The World of Biblical Literature*. New York: Basic.

Anderson, F. A. 1927. "Psychopathological Glimpses of Some Biblical Characters." *Psychoanalytic Review* 14:56–70.

Atwood, G. E., and S. S. Tomkins. 1976. "On the Subjectivity of Personality Theory." *Journal of the History of the Behavioral Sciences* 12:166-77.

Bakan, D. 1968. "Sacrifice and the Book of Job," in *Disease, Pain, and Sacrifice: Toward a Psychology of Suffering*, 95–128. Chicago: Univ. of Chicago Press.

Barton, J. 1984. *Reading the Old Testament: Method in Biblical Study*. Philadelphia: Westminster.

Bassett, R. L., K. Mathewson, and A. Galitis. 1993. "Recognizing the Person in Biblical Interpretation: An Empirical Study." *Journal of Psychology and Christianity* 12:38–46.

Bauman, M. 1988. "Shrinking Texts: the Danger of Hermeneutics Under Freudian Auspices." *Journal of the Evangelical Theological Society* 31:293–303.

Beardslee, W. A. 1993. "Poststructuralist Criticism. In *To Each Its Own Meaning: An Introduction to Biblical Criticisms and Their Application*, ed. S. L. McKenzie and S. R. Haynes, 221–35. Louisville: Westminster John Knox.

Bechtel, L. M. 1993. "Rethinking the Interpretation of Genesis 2.4b-3.24." In *A Feminist Companion to Genesis*, ed. A. Brenner, 77–117. Sheffield: Sheffield Academic.

———. 1994a. "The Adam and Eve Myth as a Myth about Human Maturation." In *The 1994 Annual of Hermeneutics and Social Concern,* ed. J. G. Lawler, 152–73. New York: Continuum.

———. 1994b. "A Psychological Approach to Genesis 2:4b-3:24." Chicago: Paper delivered to the Psychology and Biblical Studies Group, Society of Biblical Literature.

———. 1995. "Genesis 2.4b-3.24: A Myth about Human Maturation." *Journal for the Study of the Old Testament* 67:3–26.

Bleich, D. 1978. *Subjective Criticism.* Baltimore: Johns Hopkins.

———. 1988. *The Double Perspective: Language, Literacy and Social Relations.* New York: Oxford Univ. Press.

Bolin, E. P., and G. M. Goldberg. 1979. "Behavioral Psychology and the Bible: General and Specific Considerations." *Journal of Psychology and Theology* 73:167-175.

Bradshaw, J. 1981. "Oral Transmission and Human Memory." *Expository Times* 92:303–7.

Broome, E. C. 1946. "Ezekiel's Abnormal Personality." *Journal of Biblical Literature* 65:277–92.

Brown, C. A. 1981. *Jung's Hermeneutic of Doctrine: Its Theological Significance.* AAR Dissertation Series 32. Chico, Calif.: Scholars.

Bufford, R. K. 1977. "God and Behavior Mod: Some Thoughts Concerning Relationships between Biblical Principles and Behavior Modification." *Journal of Psychology and Theology* 5:13–22.

———. 1978. God and Behavior Mod: II. Some Reflections on Vos' Response. *Journal of Psychology and Theology* 6:215–18.

———. 1981. *The Human Reflex: Behavioral Psychology in Biblical Perspective.* San Francisco: Harper and Row.

Bundy, W. E. 1922. *The Psychic Health of Jesus.* New York: Macmillan.

Carroll, R. P. 1977. "Ancient Israelite Prophecy and Dissonance Theory." *Numen* 24:135–51.

———. 1980. "Prophecy and Dissonance: A Theoretical Approach to the Prophetic Tradition." *Zeitschrift für die alttestamentliche Wissenschaft* 92:108–19.

Cassem, N. H. 1973. "Ezekiel's Psychotic Personality: Reservations on the Use of the Couch for Biblical Personalities." In *Word in the World,* ed. R. Clifford, 59–68. Cambridge, Mass.: Weston College Press.

Cassuto, U. 1961. *A Commentary on the Book of Genesis: Part 1, From Adam to Noah, Genesis 1–6:8.* Trans. I. Abrahams. Jerusalem: Magnes.

Chance, S. 1987. "Ruth—An Ancient Message for Contemporary Women." *Bulletin of the Menninger Clinic* 51:373–82.

Charny, I. W. 1973. "And Abraham Went to Slay Isaac: A Parable of Killer, Victim, and Bystander in the Family of Man." *Journal of Ecumenical Studies* 10:304–18.

Clines, D. J. 1990. *What Does Eve Do to Help: And Other Readerly Questions to the Old Testament.* JSOT Supplements 94. Sheffield: JSOT.

Coan, R. W. 1973. "Toward a Psychological Interpretation of Psychology." *Journal of the History of the Behavioral Sciences* 9:313–27.

Cohen, N. J. 1983. "Two That Are One: Sibling Rivalry in Genesis." *Judaism* 32:331–42.

Cole, D. T. 1978. "A Personality Sketch of Cain, the Son of Adam." *Journal of Psychology and Theology* 6, 37–39.

Culley, R. C. 1980. Action Sequences in Genesis 2–3. *Semeia* 18:25–33.

Cunningham, A. 1991. "Psychoanalytic Approaches to Biblical Narrative Genesis 1–4." In *A Traditional Quest,* ed. D. Cohn-Sherbok, 113–32. JSOT Supplement 141. Sheffield: JSOT.

Delitzsch, F. J. 1966. *A System of Biblical Psychology* 2nd. ed. Trans. A. E. Wallis. Grand Rapids: Baker.

Diel, P. 1986a. *The God Symbol: Its History and Its Significance.* Trans. N. Marans. San Francisco: Harper and Row.

Diel, P. 1986b. *Symbolism in the Bible: The Universality of Symbolic Language and its Psychological Significance.* Trans. N. Marans. San Francisco: Harper and Row.

Dreyfus, G. 1972. "The Figures of Satan and Abraham In the Legends on Genesis 22, the Akedah." *Journal of Analytical Psychology* 17:166–78.

Dreyfus, G. 1995. *Abraham, The Man and the Symbol: A Jungian Interpretation of the Biblical Story*. Trans. Napthali Greenwood. Wilmette, Ill.: Chiron.

Driver, S. R. 1904. *The Book of Genesis. With Introduction and Notes.* 3d ed. London: Methuen.

Eco, U. 1979. *The Role of the Reader: Explorations in the Semiotics of Texts.* Bloomington: Indiana Univ. Press.

Edinger, E. F. 1972. *Ego and Archetype: Individuation and the Religious Function of the Psyche.* Baltimore: Penguin.

———. 1985. *Anatomy of the Psyche: Alchemical Symbolism in Psychotherapy.* La Salle, Ill.: Open Court.

———. 1986. *The Bible and the Psyche: Individuation Symbolism in the Old Testament.* Toronto: Inner City Books.

Fagan, J. 1976. "It Ain't Necessarily So." *Transactional Analysis Journal* 6:156–58.

Fee, G. D. 1993. *New Testament Exegesis.* Rev. ed. Louisville: Westminster John Knox.

Feldman, Y. S. 1989. "Recurrence and Sublimation: Toward a Psychoanalytic Approach to Biblical Narrative." In *Approaches to Teaching the Hebrew Bible,* ed. B. Olshen, 78–82. New York: Modern Language Association.

Fingert, H. H. 1954. "Psychoanalytic Study of the Minor Prophet, Jonah." *Psychoanalytic Review* 41:55–65.

Fiorenza, E. S. 1992. *But She Said: Feminist Practices of Biblical Interpretation.* Boston: Beacon.

Fish, S. 1980. *Is There a Text in This Class? The Authority of Interpretive Communities.* Cambridge: Harvard Univ. Press.

Fishbane, M. 1979. *Text and Texture.* New York: Schocken.

Fletcher, M. S. 1912. *The Psychology of the New Testament.* 2d ed. New York: Hodder and Stoughton.

Fodor, A. 1954. "The Fall of Man in the Book of Genesis." *American Imago* 11: 203–31.

Fortune, R. F. 1926. "The Symbolism of the Serpent." *International Journal of Psychoanalysis* 7:237–43.

Freud, S. 1953–74. *The Standard Edition of the Complete Psychological Works of Sigmund Freud,* ed. James Strachey. London: Hogarth and the Institute of Psychoanalysis. Abbreviated *SE.*

———. 1940. *An Outline of Psychoanalysis SE.* Vol. 23. London: Hogarth.

———. 1953. *The Interpretation of Dreams 1900 SE.* Vol. 4/5. London: Hogarth.

———. 1955. *Totem and Taboo 1913 SE.* Vol. 13. London: Hogarth.

———. 1959. *An Autobiographical Study 1925 SE.* Vol. 20. London: Hogarth and the Institute of Psychoanalysis.

———. 1961a. *Civilization and Its Discontents 1930 SE.* Vol. 21. London: Hogarth.

———. 1961b. *The Future of an Illusion 1927 SE.* Vol. 21. London: Hogarth.

———. 1964. *Moses and Monotheism: Three Essays 1939 SE.* Vol. 23. London: Hogarth.

Fromm, E. 1950. *Psychoanalysis and Religion.* New Haven: Yale Univ. Press.

———. 1966. *You Shall Be as Gods: A Radical Reinterpretation of the Old Testament and Its Tradition.* New York: Holt, Rinehart and Winston.

Gadamer, H.-G. 1992. *Truth and Method.* Trans. J. Weinsheimer and D. G. Marshall. 2d ed. New York: Crossroad.

Gardner, A. 1990. "Genesis 2:4b-3: A Mythological Paradigm of Sexual Equality or of the Religious History of Pre-Exilic Israel?" *Scottish Journal of Theology* 43:1–18.

Girard, R. 1987. *Job: The Victim of His People.* Trans. Y. Freccero. Stanford, Calif.: Stanford Univ. Press.

Goitein, L. 1954. "The Importance of the Book of Job for Analytic Thought." *American Imago* 11:407–15.

Goldenberg, N. 1977. "Jung after Feminism." In *Beyond Androcentrism: New Essays on Women and Religion,* ed. R. M. Gross, 53–66. Missoula, Mont.: Scholars.

Gros Louis, K. R. R. 1974. "The Garden of Eden. In *Literary Interpretations of Biblical Narratives,* ed. K. R. R. Gros Louis et al., 52–58. Nashville: Abingdon.

Gros Louis, K. R. R. 1982. "Genesis 3–11. In *Literary Interpretations of Biblical Narratives II,* ed. K. R. R. Gros Louis and J. S. Ackerman. Vol. 2, 37–52. Nashville: Abingdon.

Gruber, L. 1986. "Moses: His Speech Impediment and Behavior Therapy." *Journal of Psychology and Judaism* 10:5–13.

Gunkel, H. 1966. *Genesis. Übersetzt und erklärt.* 7th ed. Göttingen: Vanderhoeck and Ruprecht.

Hall, G. S. 1917. *Jesus, the Christ, in the Light of Psychology.* Garden City: Doubleday, Page and Co.

Halperin, D. J. 1993. *Seeking Ezekiel: Text and Psychology.* University Park: Penn State Univ. Press.

Heschel, A. J. 1962. *The Prophets*. Evanston: Harper and Row.
Hitchcock, A. W. 1907. *The Psychology of Jesus: a Study of the Development of His Self- Consciousness*. Boston: Pilgrim.
Holland, N. 1968. *The Dynamics of Literary Response*. New York: Oxford Univ. Press.
———. 1973. *Poems in Persons: An Introduction to the Psychoanalysis of Literature*. New York: Norton.
———. 1975. "Unity Identity Text Self." In *Reader-Response Criticism: From Formalism to Post-Structuralism*, ed. J. P. Tompkins, 118–33. Baltimore: Johns Hopkins Univ. Press.
———. 1975. *Readers Reading*. New Haven: Yale Univ. Press.
———. 1976. "Transactive Criticism: Re-Creation through Identity." *Criticism* 18:334–52.
———. 1990. *A Reader's Guide to Psychoanalytic Psychology and Literature-and-Psychology*. New York: Oxford Univ. Press.
Homans, P. 1969. "Psychology and Hermeneutics: Jung's Contribution." *Zygon* 44:333–55.
———. 1975. "Psychology and Hermeneutics: An Exploration of Basic Issues and Resources." *Journal of Religion and Health* 55:327–47.
———. 1979. *Jung in Context: Modernity and the Making of a Psychology*. Chicago: Univ. of Chicago Press.
———. 1989. *The Ability to Mourn: Disillusionment and the Social Origins of Psychoanalysis*. Chicago: Univ. of Chicago Press.
Iser, W. 1980. "The Reading Process: A Phenomenological Approach." In *Reader-Response Criticism: From Formalism to Post-Structuralism*, ed. J. P. Tompkins, 50–69. Baltimore: Johns Hopkins Univ. Press.
Jacobi, J. 1967. *The Way of Individuation*. Trans. R. F. C. Hull. New York: Harcourt, Brace and World.
Jacoby, M. A. 1985. *Longing for Paradise: Psychological Perspectives on an Archetype*. Trans. M. B. Gubitz. Boston: Sigo.
Jaynes, J. 1976. *The Origin of Consciousness in the Breakdown of the Bicameral Mind*. Boston: Houghton Mifflin.
Johnson, C. B. 1983. *The Psychology of Biblical Interpretation*. Grand Rapids: Zondervan.
Johnson, E. L. 1992. "A Place for the Bible within Psychological Science." *Journal of Psychology and Theology* 20:346–55.
Jork, G. 1978. "Sexualität—Eine uralte Geschichte Gen 3." In *Doppeldeutlich: Tiefendimensionen biblischer texte*, ed. Y. Spiegel, 44–56. Munich: Chr. Kaiser.
Joyce, G. C. 1910. *The Inspiration of Prophecy: An Essay in the Psychology of Religion*. New York: Oxford Univ. Press.
Jung, C. G. 1953–1979. *The Collected Works of C. G. Jung*. Ed. H. Read and M. Fordham and G. Adler Trans. R. F. C. Hull. 20 volumes. Princeton, N.J.: Princeton Univ. Press. Abbreviated *CW*.
———. 1950. "Psychology and Literature." *CW* 15:84–105. Princeton, N.J.: Princeton Univ. Press.

———. 1952. "Answer to Job." *CW* 11:355–470. Princeton, N.J.: Princeton Univ. Press.

———. 1966a. *The Spirit in Man, Art, and Literature. CW.* 2d ed. Vol. 15. Trans. R. F. C. Hull. Princeton, N.J.: Princeton Univ. Press.

———. 1966b. *Two Essays on Analytical Psychology. CW.* 2d ed. Vol. 7. R. Trans. F. C. Hull. Princeton, N.J.: Princeton Univ. Press.

———. 1967. *Symbols of Transformation. CW.* 2d ed. Vol. 5. Trans. R. F. C. Hull. Princeton, N.J.: Princeton Univ. Press.

———. 1968. *The Archetypes and the Collective Unconscious. CW.* 2d ed. Vol. 9. Trans. R. F. C. Hull. Princeton, N.J.: Princeton Univ. Press.

———. 1969. "Psychology and Religion: The Terry Lectures." *CW.* 2d ed. 11:3–105. Princeton, N.J.: Princeton Univ. Press.

———. 1971. *Psychological Types. CW.* Vol. 6. Princeton, N.J.: Princeton Univ. Press.

———. 1976a. "The Tavistock Lectures." *CW.* 18:5–182. Princeton, N.J.: Princeton Univ. Press.

———. 1976b. *The Visions Seminars.* Zurich: Spring Publications.

Jung, C. G. and M.-L. von Franz, eds. 1961. *Man and His Symbols.* New York: Doubleday.

Kaplan, J. H. 1906. "Psychology of Prophecy: a Study of the Prophetic Mind as Manifested by the Ancient Hebrew Prophets." *American Journal of Religious Psychology and Education* 169–203.

Kaplan, J. H. 1908. *Psychology of Prophecy; a Study of the Prophetic Mind as Manifested by the Ancient Hebrew Prophets.* Philadelphia: J. H. Greenstone.

Katz, R. L. 1958. "A Psychoanalytic Comment on Job 3:25." *Hebrew Union College Annual* 29:377–83.

Kelman, H. 1986. "The Day Precipitate of Pharaoh's Dreams." *Psychoanalytic Quarterly* 306–9.

Kille, D. A. 1992. "Word and Psyche: The Psychology of Religion and the Bible." *Paradigms* 72:11–19.

———. 1995. "Jacob: A Study in Individuation." In *Jung and the Interpretation of the Bible,* ed. D. L. Miller, 40–54. New York: Continuum.

Klein, W. C. 1956. *The Psychological Pattern of Old Testament Prophecy.* Evanston: Seabury-Western Theological Seminary.

Kluger, R. S. 1967. *Satan in the Old Testament.* Trans. H. Nagel. Evanston: Northwestern Univ. Press.

———. 1974. *Psyche and Bible: Three Old Testament Themes.* Zurich: Spring Publications.

Kluger, Y., and N. Kluger-Nash. 1999. *A Psychological Interpretation of Ruth.* Einseideln, Switzerland: Daimon.

Kluger-Nash, N. 1999. "Standing in the Sandals of Naomi." In *A Psychological Interpretation of Ruth,* 103–215. Einseideln, Switzerland: Daimon.

Knapp, B. L. 1984. *A Jungian Approach to Literature.* Carbondale, Ill.: Southern Illinois Univ. Press.

Koch, S., and D. E. Leary, eds. 1992. *A Century of Psychology as Science*. Washington, D.C.: American Psychological Association.

———. 1992. "The Nature and Limits of Psychological Knowledge." In *A Century of Psychology as Science,* ed. S. Koch and D. E. Leary, 75–97. Washington, D.C.: American Psychological Association.

Kühlewein, J. 1980. "Gotteserfahrung und Reifungsgeschichte in der Jakob-Esau-Erzählung." In *Werden und Wirken des Alten Testaments: Festschrift für Claus Westermann zum 70 Geburtstag,* ed. R. Albertz et al. Göttingen: Vandenhoek and Ruprecht.

Kuhn, T. S. 1970. *The Structure of Scientific Revolutions.* 2d ed. Chicago: Univ. of Chicago Press.

Landy, F. 1983. *Paradoxes of Paradise: Identity and Difference in the Song of Songs.* Sheffield: Almond.

Lawrence, C. 1983. "Redecision and Repentance: Reframing Redecision Work for the Religious Client." *Transactional Analysis Journal* 13:158–62.

Leach, E. 1969. *Genesis as Myth and Other Essays.* London: Jonathan Cape.

Levison, J. R. 1988. *Portraits of Adam in Early Judaism.* Sheffield: JSOT.

Levy, L. 1917. "Sexualsymbolik in der biblischen Paradiesgeschichte." *Imago* 5:16–30.

Lindauer, M. S. 1974. *The Psychological Study of Literature: Limitations, Possibilities, and Accomplishments.* Chicago: Nelson-Hall.

Maloney, H. N. 1985. "Psychology of Religion. In *Baker Encyclopedia of Psychology,* ed. D. G. Benner, 938–42. Grand Rapids: Baker.

Maloney, H. N., and B. Spilka, eds. 1991. *Religion in Psychodynamic Perspective: The Contributions of Paul W. Pruyser.* New York: Oxford Univ. Press.

Marotti, A. F. 1978. "Countertransference, the Communication Process, and the Dimensions of Psychoanalytic Criticism." *Critical Inquiry* 4:471–89.

McGuire, W. ed. 1974. *The Freud/Jung Letters: The Correspondence between Sigmund Freud and C. G. Jung.* Princeton: Princeton Univ. Press.

Meier, L. 1994. *Jacob.* Lanham, Md.: Univ. Press of America.

Miell, D. K. 1990. "Psychological Interpretation." In *A Dictionary of Biblical Interpretation,* ed. R. J. Coggins and J. L. Houlden, 571–72. Philadelphia: Trinity.

Milgrom, J. 1992. *Handmade Midrash.* Philadelphia: Jewish Publication Society.

Miller, J. W. 1983. "Psychoanalytic Approaches to Biblical Religion." *Journal of Religion and Health* 22:19–29.

Morris, P. 1992. "Images of Eden." In *A Walk in the Garden: Biblical, Iconographical and Literary Images of Eden,* ed. P. Morris and D. Sawyer, 21–38. Sheffield: Sheffield Academic.

Natoli, J. 1984a. *Psychocriticism: An Annotated Bibliography.* Westport, Conn: Greenwood Press.

Natoli, J. Ed.. 1984b. *Psychological Perspectives on Literature: Freudian Dissidents and Non- Freudians.* Hamden, Conn.: Archon.

Neumann, E. 1954. *The Origins and History of Consciousness.* Trans. R. F. C. Hull. Princeton: Princeton Univ. Press.

Oates, W. E. 1950. "The Diagnostic Use of the Bible: What a Man Sees in the Bible Is a Projection of His Inner Self." *Pastoral Psychology* 1:43–46.

Ong, W. 1982. "The Psychodynamics of Oral Memory and Narrative: Some Implications for Biblical Studies." In *The Pedagogy of God's Image: Essays on Symbol and the Religious Imagination*. Ed. R. Masson. Chico, Calif.: Scholars

Osiek, C. 1992. "The Social Sciences and the Second Testament." *Biblical Theological Bulletin* 22:88–95.

Pagels, E. 1988. *Adam, Eve, And the Serpent*. New York: Random House.

Parker, K. I. 1999. "Mirror, Mirror on the Wall, Must We leave Eden, Once and for All? A Lacanian Pleasure Trip through the Garden." *Journal for the Study of the Old Testament* 83:19–29.

Pfeiffer, J. et al. eds. 1989. *Literaturpsychologie 1945–1987: Eine systematische und annotierte Bibliographie*. Würzburg: Königshausen and Neumann.

Piskorowski, A. 1992. "In Search of Her Father: A Lacanian Approach to Genesis 2–3." In *A Walk in the Garden: Biblical, Iconographical and Literary Images of Eden*, ed. P. Morris and D. Sawyer, 310–18. Sheffield: Sheffield Academic.

Povah, J. W. 1924. *The New Psychology and the Bible*. London: Longmans, Green and Co.

Powell, M. A. 1992. *The Bible and Modern Literary Criticism: A Critical and Annotated Bibliography.* Bibliographies and Indexes in Religious Studies 22. Westport, Conn.: Greenwood.

———. 1991a. "Forms and Functions of the Imagination in Religion." In *Religion in Psychodynamic Perspective: the Contributions of Paul W. Pruyser*, ed. H. N. Maloney and B. Spilka, 170–88. New York: Oxford Univ. Press.

———. 1991b. "The Seamy Side of Current Religious Beliefs." In *Religion in Psychodynamic Perspective: The Contributions of Paul W. Pruyser*, ed. H. N. Maloney and B. Spilka, 47–65. New York: Oxford Univ. Press.

———. 1991c. "The Tutored Imagination in Religion." In *Religion in Psychodynamic Perspective: The Contributions of Paul W. Pruyser*, ed. H. N. Maloney and B. Spilka, 101–15. New York: Oxford Univ. Press.

Rank, O. 1922. "Völkerpsychologische Parallelen zu den infantilen Sexualtheorien." In *Psychoanalytische Beiträge zur Mythenforschung*, 43–81. Leipzig: Internationaler Psychoanalytischer Verlag.

Rashkow, I. N. 2000. *Taboo or not Taboo: Sexuality in the Hebrew Bible*. Minneapolis: Fortress Press.

Raymond, G. L. 1907. *The Psychology of Inspiration: An Attempt to Distinguish Religious from Scientific Truth and to Harmonize Christianity with Modern Thought.* New York: Funk and Wagnalls.

Reik, T. 1957. *Myth and Guilt*. New York: George Braziller.

———. 1951. "Psychoanalytic Studies of Biblical Exegesis." In *Dogma and Compulsion: Psychoanalytic Studies of Religion and Myths*, 229–75. New York: International Universities.

———. 1959. *Mystery on the Mountain: The Drama of the Sinai Revelation*. New York: Harper.

———. 1960. *The Creation of Woman: a Psychoanalytic Inquiry into the Myth of Eve*. New York: Braziller.
———. 1961. *The Temptation*. New York: George Braziller.
———. 1973. *Dogma and Compulsion: Psychoanalytic Studies of Religion and Myths*. Westport, Conn.: Greenwood.
Reynierse, J. H. 1975a. "Behavior Therapy and Job's Recovery." *Journal of Psychology and Theology* 3:187–94.
———. 1975b. "A Behavioristic Analysis of the Book of Job." *Journal of Psychology and Theology* 3:75–81.
Ricoeur, P. 1967. *The Symbolism of Evil*. Trans. E. Buchanan. Boston: Beacon.
———. 1970. *Freud and Philosophy: An Essay on Interpretation*. Trans. D. Savage. New Haven: Yale Univ. Press.
———. 1975. "Biblical Hermeneutics." *Semeia* 4:27–148.
———. 1976. *Interpretation Theory: Discourse and the Surplus of Meaning*. Fort Worth, Tx.: Texas Christian Univ. Press.
———. 1978a. "Metaphor and the Main Problem of Hermeneutics." In *The Philosophy of Paul Ricoeur: An Anthology of His Work*, ed. C. E. Reagan and D. Stewart, 134–48. Boston: Beacon.
———. 1978b. "The Question of Proof in Freud's Writings." In *The Philosophy of Paul Ricoeur: An Anthology of His Work*, ed. C. E. Reagan and D. Stewart, 184–210. Boston: Beacon.
———. 1991. "The Hermeneutical Function of Distanciation." In *From Text to Action: Essays in Hermeneutics II*, 75–88. Evanston, Ill.: Northwestern Univ. Press.
Roffey, J. W. 1987. "Genesis 3: A Foray into Psychology and Biblical Theology." *Colloquium: The Australian and New Zealand Theological Review* 192:48–56.
Rogers, M. L. 1979. "Some Biblical Families Examined from a Systems Perspective." *Journal of Psychology and Theology* 7:251–58.
Róheim, G. 1940. "The Garden of Eden." *Psychoanalytic Review* 27:1–26, 177–99.
Rollins, W. G. 1983. *Jung and the Bible*. Atlanta: John Knox Press.
———. 1985. "Jung on Scripture and Hermeneutics: Retrospect and Prospect." In *Essays on Jung and the Study of Religion*, ed. L. H. Martin and J. Goss, 81–94. Lanham, Md.: Univ. Press of America.
———. 1987. "Jung's Challenge to Biblical Hermeneutics." In *Jung's Challenge to Contemporary Religion*, ed. M. Stein and R. L. Moore, 107–26. Wilmette, Ill.: Chiron.
———. 1993. "Rationale and Agenda for a Psychological-Critical Approach to the Bible and Its Interpretation." Paper presented at Washington, D.C.: Psychology and Biblical Studies Group, Society of Biblical Literature.
———. 1995. "Psychology, Hermeneutics, and the Bible." In *Jung and the Interpretation of the Bible*, ed. D. L. Miller, 9–39. New York: Continuum.
———. 1999. *Soul and Psyche: The Bible in Psychological Perspective*. Minneapolis: Fortress Press.

Rosenberg, J. W. 1981. "The Garden Story Forward and Backward: The Non-narrative Dimension of Gen. 2–3." *Prooftexts: A Journal of Jewish Literary History* 1:1–27.

Saccuzzo, D. P. 1987. *Psychology: From Research to Applications.* Boston: Allyn and Bacon.

Sanford, J. A. 1981. "In Defense of Adam and Eve." In *The Man Who Wrestled with God: Light from the Old Testament on the Psychology of Individuation,* 115–26. Ramsey, N.J.: Paulist.

———. 1981. *The Man Who Wrestled with God: Light from the Old Testament on the Psychology of Individuation.* Ramsey, N.J.: Paulist.

———. 1985. *King Saul, the Tragic Hero: A Study in Individuation.* New York: Paulist.

Schleiermacher, F. D. E. 1974. *Hermeneutics: The Handwritten Manuscripts by F.D.E. Schleiermacher.* Trans. J. Duke and J. Forstman. Heidelberg: Carl Winter.

Schneidau, H. N. 1986. "Biblical Narrative and Modern Consciousness." In *The Bible and the Narrative Tradition,* ed. F. McConnell, 132–50. New York: Oxford Univ. Press.

Schneiders, S. 1991. *The Revelatory Text.* San Francisco: HarperSanFrancisco.

Schweitzer, A. 1948. *The Psychiatric Study of Jesus: Exposition and Criticism.* Trans. C. R. Joy. Boston: Beacon.

Scroggs, R. 1982. "Psychology as a Tool to Interpret the Text." *Christian Century* (March 24) 335–38.

Shepperson, V. L. 1984. "Jacob's Journey: From Narcissism toward Wholeness." *Journal of Psychology and Theology* 12:178–87.

Shiryon, M. 1992. "The Stories of Exodus as Metaphors for Psychotherapy." *Journal of Psychology and Judaism* 16:235–44.

Sigal, L. 1990. "The Feminine Divine in the Book of Esther: A Psychoanalytic Study." In *The Bible in Light of Cuneiform Literature: Scripture in Context III,* ed. W. Hallo et al., 381–411. Lewiston: Mellen.

Stein, D. 1980. "Is Psycho-Analytic Reading of the Bible Possible?" In *Conflicting Ways of Interpreting the Bible,* ed. H. Küng and J. Moltmann, 24–32. New York: Seabury.

Stein, M. 1985. *Jung's Treatment of Christianity: The Psychotherapy of a Religious Tradition.* Wilmette, Ill.: Chiron.

Stendhal, K. 1976. "The Apostle Paul and the Introspective Conscience of the West." In *Paul Among Jews and Gentiles,* 78–96. Philadelphia: Fortress Press.

Steyn, J. 1984. "Some Psycholinguistic Factors Involved in the Discourse Analysis of Ancient Texts." *Theologia Evangelica* 172:51–65.

Sugg, R. P., ed. 1992. *Jungian Literary Criticism.* Evanston, Ill.: Northwestern Univ. Press.

Theissen, G. 1975. "The Sociological Interpretation of Religious Traditions: Its Methodological Problems as Exemplified in Early Christianity." In *The Social*

Setting of Pauline Christianity: Essays on Corinth, 175–200. Trans. J. H. Schütz. Philadelphia: Fortress Press.

———. 1987. *Psychological Aspects of Pauline Theology*. Trans. J. P. Galvin. Philadelphia: Fortress Press.

Thiselton, A. C. 1980. *The Two Horizons: New Testament Hermeneutics and Philosophical Description with Special Reference to Heidegger, Bultmann, Gadamer, and Wittgenstein*. Grand Rapids: Eerdmans.

———. 1992. *New Horizons in Hermeneutics*. London: HarperCollins.

Thomas, D. E. 1914. *The Psychological Approach to the Study of Prophecy*. Unpublished Ph.D., Chicago.

Trible, P. 1978. *God and the Rhetoric of Sexuality*. Overtures to Biblical Theology. Philadelphia: Fortress Press.

Van Praag, H. M. 1986. "The Downfall of King Saul: The Neurobiological Consequences of Losing Hope." *Judaism* 354:414–28.

Vande Kemp, H. 1986. "Dangers of Psychologism: The Place of God in Psychology." *Journal of Psychology and Theology* 14:97–109.

Vitz, P. C. 1985. "Psychology as Religion." In *Baker Encyclopedia of Psychology*, ed. D. G. Benner, 932–38. Grand Rapids: Baker.

Vogels, W. 1981. "The Spiritual Growth of Job: A Psychological Approach to the Book of Job." *Biblical Theology Bulletin* 11:77–80.

———. 1983. "The Inner Development of Job: One More Look at Psychology and the Book of Job." *Science et Esprit* 35:227–30.

Vonck, P. 1984. "The Crippling Victory: The Story of Jacob's Struggle at the River Jabbok Genesis 32:23-33." *AFER* 26:75–87.

Walsh, J. A. 1983. "The Dream of Joseph: A Jungian Interpretation." *Journal of Psychology and Theology* 11:20–27.

Watt, I. 1995. "Joseph's Dreams." In *Jung and the Interpretation of the Bible*, ed. D. L. Miller, 55–70. New York: Continuum.

Wehr, D. 1987. *Jung and Feminism: Liberating Archetypes*. Boston: Beacon.

Westman, H. 1961. *The Springs of Creativity*. London: Routledge and Kegan Paul.

———. 1983. *The Structure of Biblical Myths: the Ontogenesis of the Psyche*. Dallas, Tx.: Spring.

Wink, W. 1973. *The Bible in Human Transformation: Toward a New Paradigm for Biblical Study*. Philadelphia: Fortress Press.

———. 1978. "On Wrestling with God: Using Psychological Insights in Bible Study." *Religion in Life* 47:136–47.

———. 1980. *Transforming Bible Study: A Leader's Guide*. Nashville: Abingdon.

Wohlgelernter, D. K. 1988. "Goal Directedness: Understanding the Development of the Book of Job." *Individual Psychology: Journal of Adlerian Theory, Research* and *Practice* 44:296–306.

van Wolde, E. J. 1989. *A Semiotic Analysis of Genesis 2-3: A Semiotic Theory and Method of Analysis Applied to the Story of the Garden of Eden*. Studia Semitica Nederlandica 25. Assen: Van Gorcum.

Wood, F. B. 1988. "A Neuropsychological Commentary on Biblical Faith." In *Civil Religion and Transcendent Experience,* ed. R. Wood, 129–35. Macon, Ga.: Mercer Univ. Press.

Wright, E. D. 1909. *The Psychology of Christ.* New York: Cochrane.

Wuellner, W., and R. Leslie. 1984. *The Surprising Gospel: Intriguing Psychological Insights from the New Testament.* Nashville: Abingdon.

Wulff, D. M. 1985. "Psychological Approaches." In *Contemporary Approaches to the Study of Religion, Vol. 2: The Social Sciences.* ed. F. Whaling, 21–88. Berlin: Mouton.

———. 1991–92. "Reality, Illusion, or Metaphor? Reflections on the Conduct and Object of the Psychology of Religion." *Newsletter, Psychologists Interested in Religious Issues, APA Division* 36:171, 1–9.

Zabriskie, C. 1976. "A Psychological Analysis of Biblical Interpretations Pertaining to Women." *Journal of Psychology and Theology* 4:304–12.

Zeligs, D. 1974. *Psychoanalysis and the Bible: A Study in Depth of Seven Leaders.* New York: Bloch.

———. 1986. *Moses: A Psychodynamic Study.* New York: Human Sciences Press.

FOR ADDITIONAL READING

General Studies

Bonchek, A. 1996. *Studying the Torah: A Guide to In-Depth Interpretation.* Northvale, N.J.: Jason Aronson.

Capps, D. 1984. "The Bible's Role in Pastoral Care and Counseling: Four Basic Principles." *Journal of Psychology and Christianity* 34:5–15.

Corey, L. 1988. "Gates of Righteousness: Prologue to a Model of Analytical Torah Psychology." *Tiferet: The International Journal of Archetypal Torah Psychology* 1:1–33.

Cronbach, A. 1931–32. "The Psychoanalytic Study of Judaism." *Hebrew Union College Annual,* 8–9, 605–740.

Dallett, J. 1982. "Active Imagination in Practice." In *Jungian Analysis,* ed. M. Stein, 173–91. Boston: New Science Library.

Edinger, E. 1984. *The Creation of Consciousness: Jung's Myth for Modern Man.* Toronto: Inner City.

Edinger, E. 1992. *Transformation of the God-Image: An Elucidation of Jung's "Answer to Job."* Toronto: Inner City.

Erikson, E. H. 1950. *Childhood and Society.* 2d ed. New York: Norton.

———. 1982. *The Life Cycle Completed: A Review.* New York: Norton.

Freud, S. 1966. *Introductory Lectures on Psychoanalysis,* trans. J. Strachey. New York: Norton.

Gilligan, C. 1982. *In a Different Voice: Psychological Theory and Women's Development.* Cambridge: Harvard Univ. Press.

Jacobi, J. 1971. *The Psychology of C.G. Jung*. Rev. ed. New Haven: Yale Univ. Press.
Kings, S. 1997. "Jung's Hermeneutics of Scripture." *Journal of Religion* 77:233–51.
Kohlberg, L. 1984. *The Psychology of Moral Development: Nature and Validity of Moral Stages*. San Francisco: Harper and Row.
Kohut, H. 1971. *The Analysis of the Self*. New York: International Universities Press.
Meier, L. 1991. *Jewish Values in Jungian Psychology*. Lanham, Md.: Univ. Press of America.
Rabinowitz, A. 1999. *Judaism and Psychology: Meeting Points*. Northvale, N.J.: Jason Aaronson, Inc.
Reagan, C. E. 1979. Psychoanalysis as Hermeneutics. In *Studies in the Philosophy of Paul Ricoeur*, ed. C. E. Reagan, 141–61. Athens: Ohio Univ. Press.
Rubenstein, R. 1968. *The Religious Imagination: A Study in Psychoanalysis and Jewish Theology*. Indianapolis: Bobbs-Merrill.
Spiegelman, J. M. 1992. *Judaism and Jungian Psychology*. Lanham, Md.: University Press of America.
Vande Kemp, H. and H. N. Malony, eds. 1984. *Psychology and Theology in Western Thought: A Historical and Annotated Bibliography*. Millwood, N.Y.: Kraus International.
Weisstub, E. 1993. "Questions to Jung on 'Answer to Job.'" *Journal of Analytical Psychology* 384:397–418.
Welland, M. 1997. "Active imagination in Jung's Answer to Job." *Studies in Religion/Sciences religieuses* 3:297–308.
Zeligs, D. 1957. "A Psychoanalytic Note on the Function of the Bible." *American Imago* 14:57–60.

Psychology and Literature

Bedford, G. 1978. "Freud and Hermeneutics: Notes on the Overdetermination of Meaning in the Psyche." *Journal of the American Academy of Religion* 46:361.
Berman, E., ed. 1993. *Essential Papers on Literature and Psychoanalysis*. New York: New York Univ. Press.
Brooks, P. 1987. "The Idea of Psychoanalytic Criticism. In *Discourse in Psychoanalysis and Literature*, ed. S. Rimmon-Kenan. London: Methuen.
Coles, R. 1980. "Commentary on 'Psychology and Literature'." *New Literary History* 12:207–11.
Hallman, R. J. 1961. *Psychology of Literature: A Study of Alienation and Tragedy*. New York: Philosophical Library.
Holland, N. 1982. "Why This Is Transference, Nor Am I Out of It. *Psychoanalysis and Contemporary Thought* 5:27–34.
———. 1990. *A Reader's Guide to Psychoanalytic Psychology and Literature-and-Psychology*. New York: Oxford Univ. Press.
Jacobs, A. 1991. "Psychological Criticism: From the Imagination to Freud and Beyond." In *Contemporary Literary Theory: A Christian Appraisal*, ed. C. Walhout and L. Ryken, 94–124. Grand Rapids, Mich.: Eerdmans.

Jung, C. G. 1931. "On the Relation of Analytical Psychology to Poetry." 2d ed., *CW* 15:65–83. Princeton, N.J.: Princeton Univ. Press.

Kiell, N. 1990. *Psychoanalysis, Psychology and Literature: A Bibliography*. Madison: Univ. Press of Wisconsin.

Kristeva, J. 1980. *Desire In Language: A Semiotic Approach to Literature and Art.* Trans. T. Gora, A. Jardine, and L. S. Roudicz. New York: Columbia Univ. Press.

Kurzweil, E., and W. Phillips, eds. 1983. *Literature and Psychoanalysis*. New York: Columbia Univ. Press.

Payne, M. 1993. *Reading Theory: An Introduction to Lacan, Derrida, and Kristeva* . Oxford, U.K.; Cambridge, Mass.: Blackwell.

Philipson, M. 1963. *Outline of a Jungian Aesthetics*. Evanston, Ill.: Northwestern Univ. Press.

Reppen, J. and M. Charney, ed. 1985. *Psychoanalytic Study of Literature.*

———. 1987. *Psychoanalytic Approaches to Literature and Film.*

Rimmon-Kenan, S., ed. 1987. *Discourse in Psychoanalysis and Literature.* London: Methuen.

Schwartz, M. M. 1980. "Introduction Psychology and Literature." *New Literary History* 12:1–9.

Snider, C. 1977. "C. G. Jung's Analytical Psychology and Literary Criticism II." *Psychocultural Review* 12:216–42.

Tennenhouse, L., ed. 1976. *The Practice of Psychoanalytic Criticism*. Detroit, Mich.: Wayne State Univ. Press.

Van Meurs, J., ed. 1988. *Jungian Literary Criticism 1920–1980: An Annotated, Critical Bibliography of Works in English with a selection of titles after 1980*. Metuchen, N.J.: Scarecrow.

von Franz, M.-L. 1980. "Analytical Psychology and Literary Criticism." *New Literary History* 12:119–26.

Wright, E. 1984. *Psychoanalytic Criticism: Theory in Practice*. New York: Methuen.

Studies of Biblical Texts and Themes

Achenbaum, W. A., and L. Orwoll, 1991. "Becoming Wise: A Psycho-gerontological Interpretation of the Book of Job." *International Journal of Aging and Human Development* 32:21–39.

Andreson, J. J. 1991. "Biblical Job: Changing the Helper's Mind." *Contemporary Psychoanalysis* 27:454–81.

Bal, M. 1987. *Lethal Love: Feminist Literary Readings of Biblical Love Stories*. Bloomington, Ind.: Indiana Univ. Press.

Barak, Y., and A. Achiron, 1998. "Age-Related Disorders in the Bible." *Aging and Mental Health* 24:275–78.

Bennett, B. M. 1978. "Vision and Audition in Biblical Prophecy." *Parapsychology Review* 9:1–12.

Berman, L. A. 1997. "Isaac and Oedipus." In *The Akedah: The Binding of Isaac,* 159–71. Northvale, N.J.: Jason Aaronson.

Bruns, J. E. 1959. "Depth-Psychology and the Fall." *Catholic Biblical Quarterly* 21:78–82.

Bugg, C. B. 1998. "Joshua 24:14-18—The Choice." *Review and Expositor* 95:279–84.

Burston, D. 1994. "Freud, the Serpent, and the Sexual Enlightenment of Children." *International Forum of Psychoanalysis* 34:205–19.

Cooper, H. J. 1991. "Guilt and God, or 'Whatever Happened in the Garden?'" *Journal of Psychology and Judaism* 15:75–88.

Cranmer, D. J., and B. E. Eck, 1994. "God Said It: Psychology and Biblical Interpretation, How Text and Reader Interact Through the Glass Darkly." *Journal of Psychology and Theology* 223:207–14.

Dailey, T. F. 1997. "The Wisdom of Job : Moral Maturity or Religious Reckoning." *Union Seminary Quarterly Review* 1–2.

Davis, R. H. 1997. "Calling a Divine Summons: Biblical and Depth Psychological Perspectives." *Union Seminary Quarterly Review* 3–4.

Derby, J. 1996. "A Biblical Freudian Slip: II Samuel 12:6." *Jewish Bible Quarterly* 24 (April–June) 107–11.

Drewek, P. A. 1991. "Adam and Eve Revisited and Revised." *Anima* 18:9–25.

Edinger, E. F. 1999. *Archetype of the Apocalypse: A Jungian Study of the Book of Revelation*. Chicago: Open Court.

Edinger, E. F. J. G. and Sparks. 2000. *Ego and Self: The Old Testament Prophets—From Isaiah to Malachi*. Toronto, Canada: Inner City.

Ellens, J. H. 1997. "The Bible and Psychology, an Interdisciplinary Pilgrimage." *Pastoral Psychology* 45:193–208.

———. 1997. "A Psychodynamic Hermeneutic of the Fall Story: Genesis 2:25-3:24 Through a Psychological Lens." *Pastoral Psychology* 45:221–36.

———. 1997. "Psychology and the Bible: The Interface of Corollary Disciplines." *Pastoral Psychology* 45:159–62.

Gladson, J. A. 1992. "Higher Than the Heavens: Forgiveness in the Old Testament." *Journal of Psychology and Christianity* 11:125–35.

Gladson, J. A. and R. Lucas. 1989. "Hebrew Wisdom and Psychotheological Dialogue." *Zygon* 24:357–76.

Gladson, J. A. and C. Plott. 1991. "Unholy Wedlock? The Peril and Promise of Applying Psychology to the Bible." *Journal of Psychology and Christianity* 101:54–64.

Goodnick, B. 1991. "The Oedipus Complex and its Biblical Parallels." *Jewish Biblical Quarterly* 201:24–34.

Grant, F. C. 1968. "Psychological Study of the Bible." In *Religions in Antiquity: Essays in Memory of Erwin Goodenough*, ed. J. Neusner, 107–24. Leiden: Brill.

Gregory, S. 1980. *A New Dimension in Old Testament Study: A Course guide to the Study of Selections from the Old Testament for Individuals and Groups*. San Francisco: Guild for Psychological Studies.

Greven, P. J. 1991. *Spare the Child: The Religious Roots of Punishment and the Psychological Impact of Physical Abuse*. New York: Knopf.

Gubitz, M. B. 1977. "Amalek: The Eternal Adversary." *Psychological Perspectives* 8:34–58.

Kaplan, K. J. and D. Algom. 1997. "Freud, Oedipus and the Hebrew Bible." *Journal of Psychology and Judaism* 21:211–16.

———. and M. B. Schwartz. 1998. "Jacob's Blessing and the Curse of Oedipus: Sibling Rivalry and Its Resolution." *Journal of Psychology and Judaism* 22:71–84.

Kluger, R. S. 1995. *Psyche in Scripture: "The Idea of the Chosen People" and Other Essays*. Toronto, Canada: Inner City.

Knapp, B. L. 1995. *Manna and Mystery: A Jungian Approach to Hebrew Myth and Legend*. Wilmette, Ill.: Chiron.

Kramer, D. and M. Moore. 1998. "Sour Grapes: Transgenerational Family Pathology in the Hebrew Bible." *Journal of Psychology and Judaism* 22:65–69.

Kristeva, J. 1974. *About Chinese Women*. New York: Marion Boyers. [Includes a lengthy meditation on Adam and Eve.]

L'Heureux, C. E. 1983. *In and Out of Paradise: The Book of Genesis from Adam and Eve to the Tower of Babel*. New York: Paulist.

———. 1986. *Life Journey and the Old Testament: An Experiential Approach to the Bible and Personal Transformation*. New York: Paulist.

Lacocque, A. and P.-E. Lacocque. 1990. *Jonah: A Psycho-Religious Approach to the Prophet*. Columbia: Univ. Press of South Carolina Press.

Lemaigre, B. 1992. "'Thou Shalt Not Make unto Thee Any Graven Images . . .' Exodus 20:4: Reflections on the Biblical Interdiction to Make Images and Its Psychoanalytic Interpretation." *Revue Francaise de Psychanalyse* 561:237–50.

Lewin, I. 1983. "The Psychological Theory of Dreams in the Bible." *Journal of Psychology and Judaism* 72:73–88.

Luke, H. M. 1982. *The Inner Story: Myth and Symbol in the Bible and Literature*. New York: Crossroad.

Lynch, T. H. 1971. "Corroboration of Jungian Psychology in the Biblical Story of Abraham." *Psychotherapy: Theory, Research* and *Practice* 8:315–18.

Maas, J. P. 1989. "A Psychological Assessment of Job." *Pacific Journal of Theology* 21:55–68.

Mann, D. 1992. "The Infantile Origins of the Creation and Apocalyptic Myths." *International Review of Psycho-Analysis* 194:471–82.

Marcus, P. 2000. "The Wisdom of Ecclesiastes and Its Meaning for Psychoanalysis." *Psychoanalytic Review* 872:227–50.

Mazor, Y. 1986. "Genesis 22: The Ideological Rhetoric and the Psychological Composition." *Biblica* 67:81–88.

McElroy, B. L. 1915. "The Psychological Truth of the Bible." *Methodist Review* 97:772–76.

Meier, L. 1996. *Ancient Secrets: Using the Stories of the Bible to Improve Our Everyday Lives*. New York: Village.

Merkur, D. 1985. "The Prophecies of Jeremiah." *American Imago* 421:137.

———. 1988. "Prophetic Initiation in Israel and Judah." In *The Psychoanalytic Study of Society*, ed. L. B. Boyer and S. A. Grolnick, 37–67. Hillsdale, N.J.: Analytic.

———. 1988. "The Visionary Practices of Jewish Apocalyptists." In *The Psychoanalytic Study of Society*, ed. L. B. Boyer and S. A. Grolnick, 119–48. Hillsdale, N.J.: Analytic.

Meves, C. 1977. "Expulsion as Motivation for Maturation: A Depth Psychological Interpretation of the Fall Gen. 3:1-24." *The Bible Answers Us with Pictures*, 17–29. Philadelphia: Westminster.

Meyer, S. G. 1974. "The Psalms and Personal Counseling." *Journal of Psychology and Theology* 2:26–30.

Miller, D. L., ed.. 1995. *Jung and the Interpretation of the Bible*. New York: Continuum.

More, J. 1970. "The Prophet Jonah: the Story of an Intrapsychic Process." *American Imago* 27:3–11.

Morrow, W. S. 1998. "Toxic Religion and the Daughters of Job." *Studies in Religion/Sciences religieuses* 3:263–76.

Moseley, J. G. 1983. "Innerantism as Narcissism: Biblical Authority as a Cultural Problem." *Perspectives in Religious Studies* 103:203–13.

Mumford, D. B. 1992. "Emotional distress in the Hebrew Bible: Somatic or psychological?" *British Journal of Psychiatry* 160:92–97.

North, R. 1982. "David's Rise: Sacral, Military, or Psychiatric?" *Biblica* 63:524–44.

Orbach, I. 1994. "Job—A Biblical Message About Suicide." *Journal of Psychology and Judaism* 18:241–47.

Phillips, J. A. 1984. *Eve: The History of an Idea*. San Francisco: Harper and Row.

Pilch, J. J. 1997. "Psychological and Psychoanalytical Approaches to Interpreting the Bible in Social-Scientific Context." *Biblical Theology Bulletin* 27:112–16.

Pitzele, P. A. 1991. "The Psychodrama of the Bible: Mirror and Window of Soul." *Religious Education* 86:562–70.

———. 1995. *Our fathers' Wells: A Personal Encounter with the Myths of Genesis*. San Francisco: HarperSanFrancisco.

Powlison, D. A. 1984. "Which Presuppositions? Secular Psychology and the Categories of Biblical Thought." *Journal of Psychology and Theology* 12:270–78.

Putscher, M. 1982. "Dreams and Dream Interpretation in the Bible." *Israel Journal of Psychiatry and Related Sciences* 19:149–55.

Rabin, A. I. 1998. *Psychological issues in Biblical lore: Explorations in the Old Testament*. New York, N.Y.: Springer.

Randolph, R. M. 1988. "The Burning Bush: Art and the Individuation of God." *Journal of Evolutionary Psychology* 93–94:230–35.

Rashkow, I. N. 1992. "Intertextuality, Transference and the Reader in/of the Biblical Text." In *Reading Between Texts*, ed. D. N. Fewell, 57–73. Louisville: Westminster John Knox.

———. 1993. "Daughters and Fathers in Genesis . . . Or, What Is Wrong with This Picture?" In *New Literary Criticism and the Bible,* ed. J. C. Exum and D. Clines. Sheffield: Sheffield Academic.

———. 1993. *The Phallacy of Genesis: a Feminist-Psychoanalytic Approach.* Louisville: Westminster John Knox.

Renik, O. 1991. "The Biblical Book of Job: Advice to Clinicians." *Psychoanalytic Quarterly* 60:596–606.

Robinson, H. W. 1946. "The Psychology of Inspiration." *Inspiration and Revelation in the Old Testament.* Oxford: Clarendon.

Rollins, W. G. 1997. "The Bible and Psychology: New Directions in Biblical Scholarship." *Pastoral Psychology* 45:163–79.

Rosenblatt, N. H. 1995. *Wrestling with Angels: What Genesis Teaches Us About Our Spiritual Identity, Sexuality, and Personal Relationships.* New York: Delta/ Dell.

Sanford, J. A. 1984. "Kunkel's Psychology and the Bible." In *Fritz Kunkel: Selected Writings,* ed. J. A. Sanford, 333–52. New York: Paulist.

Sauve, J. R. 1992. "Joshua: A Story of Individuation." *Journal of Religion and Health* 31:265–71.

Savage, J. C. 1999. *Psychotherapy and Exegesis: A Study of Parallel Processes.* The Union Inst, US.

Schimmel, S. 1987. "Job and the Psychology of Suffering and Doubt." *Journal of Psychology and Judaism* 11:239–49.

Selinger, S. 1994. "Moses: 'Kill Me, I Pray'." *Journal of Psychology and Judaism* 18:231–39.

Seller, S. C. 1985. "Alcohol Abuse in the Old Testament." *Alcohol and Alcoholism* 20:69–76.

Sexton, R. O. and R. C. Maddock. 1984. "The Adam and Eve Syndrome Revisited." *Medical Hypnoanalysis* 5:152–56.

Stein, C. 1976. "Psychotherapy in the Bible." *Journal of the American Academy of Psychiatry and Neurology* 1:67–70.

Strunk, O. 1956. "Psychology, Religion, and C. G. Jung: A Review of Periodical Literature." *Journal of Bible and Religion* 24:106–13.

Trible, P. 1979. "Eve and Adam: Genesis 2–3 Reread." In *Womanspirit Rising: A Feminist Reader in Religion,* ed. C. P. Christ and J. Plaskow, 74–83. San Francisco: Harper and Row.

Weber, M. 1967. "Judaism: The Psychology of the Prophets." In *Propaganda and Communication in World History, vol. I,* ed. H. D. Lesswell and D. Lerner and H. Speier, 299–329. Honolulu: Univ. Press of Hawaii.

Weiss, A. 1994. "Jacob's Struggle: A Psycho-Existential Exegesis." *Journal of Psychology and Judaism* 18:19–31.

Wellisch, E. 1955. *Isaac and Oedipus: a Study in Biblical Psychology of the Sacrifice of Isaac, the Akedah.* New York: Humanities.

Widengren, G. 1948. *Literary and Psychological Aspects of the Hebrew Prophets.* Vol. 10. Uppsala, Sweden: A.-B. Lundequistska.

Wiener, A. 1978. *The Prophet Elijah in the Development of Judaism: A Depth Psychological Study*. London: Routledge and Kegan Paul.

Zeligs, D. F. 1973. "Moses and Pharaoh: A Psychoanalytic Study of their Encounter." *American Imago* 30:192–220.

Zeligs, D. F. 1996. "The Family Romance of Moses." *American Imago* 232:110–31.

Zevit, Z. 1990. "Roman Jakobson, Psycholinguistics, and Biblical Poetry." *Journal of Biblical Literature* 109:385–401.